Sho
Disabled Supporters' Guide to British Football 1995

EDITOR
John Robinson

First Edition

British Library Cataloguing in Publication Data

A catalogue record for this book is available from the British Library

ISBN 0-947808-40-X

72, St. Peters' Avenue, Cleethorpes, Sth. Humberside, DN35 8HU, England

The Publishers, and the Football Clubs itemised are unable to accept liability for any loss, damage or injury caused by error or inaccuracy in the information published in this guide.

Printed by Adlard Print & Typesetting Services, The Old School, The Green, Ruddington, Notts. NG11 6HH

Disabled Information

The information shown in this section was provided by the clubs and is as complete as possible. Although the number of spaces for wheelchairs can be very limited, most clubs will endeavour to accommodate wheelchair users even if the spaces have already been filled but, in every case, we advise a telephone enquiry at least 7 days before the game.

Disabled supporters (other than wheelchair users) may experience difficulty in obtaining discretionary 'disabled' entry rates, as some clubs seem to regard wheelchair users alone as qualifying for reduced or free rates where applicable.

A final word of warning - a number of clubs are in the process of revamping their disabled facilities and the information shown below may therefore change for those clubs. Once again, we emphasise that if any points remain unclear, please contact the club in question *at least* 7 days before the game.

F.A. Carling Premiership & Football League Clubs

Arsenal FC

Wheelchairs : **Location of Accommodation**: Disabled Section, Lower Tier East Stand
Nº Spaces for Home Fans; Nº Spaces for Away Fans: 20 spaces available in total
Are Helpers Admitted; Nº Admitted: One Helper admitted per Wheelchair. 20 in total.
Prices : **Prices for Disabled; Prices for Helpers**: Free of Charge
Toilets : **Location of Disabled Toilets (+ Number)**: 3 in South Stand. One in Lower East 'H' block
Blind : **Facilities Available**: Commentaries Available
Bookings : **Are Bookings Necessary**: Yes **Contact Number**: (071) 226-0304

Aston Villa FC

Wheelchairs : **Location of Accommodation**: Special Section - Trinity Road Stand
Nº Spaces for Home Fans; Nº Spaces for Away Fans: 40 Spaces in total
Are Helpers Admitted; Nº Admitted: By letter of request of disabled - one per disabled fan.
Prices : **Prices for Disabled; Prices for Helpers**: At Club's discretion for disabled. Helpers full price.
Toilets : **Location of Disabled Toilets (+ Number)**: One in Trinity Road Stand
Blind : **Facilities Available**: Commentaries by Arrangement
Bookings : **Are Bookings Necessary**: Yes **Contact Number**: (021) 327-2299

Barnet FC

Wheelchairs : **Location of Accommodation**: Main Stand - Barnet Lane Entrance (Social Club End)
Nº Spaces for Home Fans; Nº Spaces for Away Fans: 12 Spaces in Total
Are Helpers Admitted; Nº Admitted: One helper admitted per wheelchair
Prices : **Prices for Disabled; Prices for Helpers**: Contact club for details
Toilets : **Location of Disabled Toilets (+ Number)**: One in Social Club
Blind : **Facilities Available**: No Special Facilities
Bookings : **Are Bookings Necessary**: Yes **Contact Number**: (081) 441-6932

Barnsley FC

Wheelchairs : **Location of Accommodation**: Accommodated in Disabled Stand (Left of Main Stand)
Nº Spaces for Home Fans; Nº Spaces for Away Fans: 55 Spaces in Total
Are Helpers Admitted; Nº Admitted: Yes; Depends on Opponents
Prices : **Prices for Disabled; Prices for Helpers**: Disabled admitted free. Helpers £6.50
Toilets : **Location of Disabled Toilets (+ Number)**: Adjacent to Disabled Stand
Blind : **Facilities Available**: Commentaries Available
Bookings : **Are Bookings Necessary**: Usually Not **Contact Number**: (0226) 295353

Birmingham City FC

Wheelchairs : **Location of Accommodation**: Remploy Stand
Nº Spaces for Home Fans; Nº Spaces for Away Fans: Pass Holders (Away Fans please ring)
Are Helpers Admitted; Nº Admitted: One helper admitted per wheelchair
Prices : **Prices for Disabled; Prices for Helpers**: Free of Charge for each disabled person & helper
Toilets : **Location of Disabled Toilets (+ Number)**: One available in Remploy Stand
Blind : **Facilities Available**: No Special Facilities
Bookings : **Are Bookings Necessary**: No **Contact Number**: (021) 772-0101

Blackburn Rovers FC

Wheelchairs : **Location of Accommodation**: Disabled Section in Walkersteel Stand
Nº Spaces for Home Fans; Nº Spaces for Away Fans: 44 spaces in total but more being built
Are Helpers Admitted; Nº Admitted: One helper admitted per disabled supporter
Prices : **Prices for Disabled; Prices for Helpers**: Free of Charge for both disabled & helpers
Toilets : **Location of Disabled Toilets (+ Number)**: In Disabled Section
Blind : **Facilities Available**: Commentaries Available by Arrangement for up to 6 people
Bookings : **Are Bookings Necessary**: Yes **Contact Number**: (0254) 698888

Blackpool FC

Wheelchairs : **Location of Accommodation**: In South Paddock
Nº Spaces for Home Fans; Nº Spaces for Away Fans: 12 Spaces in total
Are Helpers Admitted; Nº Admitted: One helper admitted per disabled supporter
Prices : **Prices for Disabled; Prices for Helpers**: Free of Charge for both disabled & helpers
Toilets : **Location of Disabled Toilets (+ Number)**: None
Blind : **Facilities Available**: Headphone Commentaries Available in South Stand for three people
Bookings : **Are Bookings Necessary**: Yes **Contact Number**: (0253) 404331

Bolton Wanderers FC

Wheelchairs : **Location of Accommodation**: Manchester Road Paddock
Nº Spaces for Home Fans; Nº Spaces for Away Fans: 4 spaces each for Home & Away fans
Are Helpers Admitted; Nº Admitted: One helper admitted per disabled person
Prices : **Prices for Disabled; Prices for Helpers**: Free of charge for Wheelchairs. Helpers full-price
Toilets : **Location of Disabled Toilets (+ Number)**: One available in Disabled Area
Blind : **Facilities Available**: No Special Facilities
Bookings : **Are Bookings Necessary**: No **Contact Number**: (0204) 389200

AFC Bournemouth

Wheelchairs : **Location of Accommodation**: Accommodated by Prior Arrangement - South Stand
Nº Spaces for Home Fans; Nº Spaces for Away Fans: 16 Spaces in total
Are Helpers Admitted; Nº Admitted: One helper admitted per disabled person
Prices : **Prices for Disabled; Prices for Helpers**: Free of Charge for both disabled & helpers
Toilets : **Location of Disabled Toilets (+ Number)**: One in South Stand - adjacent to Disabled Section
Blind : **Facilities Available**: No Special Facilities
Bookings : **Are Bookings Necessary**: Yes **Contact Number**: (0202) 395381

Bradford City FC

Wheelchairs : **Location of Accommodation**: 'A' Block, N & P Stand
Nº Spaces for Home Fans; Nº Spaces for Away Fans: 40 Spaces available in total
Are Helpers Admitted; Nº Admitted: One helper admitted per disabled person
Prices : **Prices for Disabled; Prices for Helpers**: Both disabled fans and helpers admitted half-price
Toilets : **Location of Disabled Toilets (+ Number)**: One behind disabled section
Blind : **Facilities Available**: No Special Facilities
Bookings : **Are Bookings Necessary**: Yes **Contact Number**: (0274) 306062

BRENTFORD FC

WHEELCHAIRS : **Location of Accommodation**: Disabled Section - Braemar Road
Nº Spaces for Home Fans; Nº Spaces for Away Fans: 30 spaces available in total
Are Helpers Admitted; Nº Admitted: One helper admitted per disabled person
PRICES : **Prices for Disabled; Prices for Helpers**: Free of charge for both the disabled and helpers.
TOILETS : **Location of Disabled Toilets (+ Number)**: One each (male & female) Braemar Road
BLIND : **Facilities Available**: Commentaries Available in Braemar Road Stand
BOOKINGS : **Are Bookings Necessary**: Yes **CONTACT NUMBER**: (081) 560-6062

BRIGHTON & HOVE ALBION FC

WHEELCHAIRS : **Location of Accommodation**: Disabled Section - S.W. Corner of Ground
Nº Spaces for Home Fans; Nº Spaces for Away Fans: 20 spaces available in total
Are Helpers Admitted; Nº Admitted: One helper admitted per disabled person. Seats nearby
PRICES : **Prices for Disabled; Prices for Helpers**: Disabled free of charge - helpers £6.00
TOILETS : **Location of Disabled Toilets (+ Number)**: One in the disabled section
BLIND : **Facilities Available**: Commentaries Available in West Stand
BOOKINGS : **Are Bookings Necessary**: Yes **CONTACT NUMBER**: (0273) 778855

BRISTOL CITY FC

WHEELCHAIRS : **Location of Accommodation**: Accommodated at Pitchside
Nº Spaces for Home Fans; Nº Spaces for Away Fans: Limited Number - please apply early
Are Helpers Admitted; Nº Admitted: One helper admitted per disabled person
PRICES : **Prices for Disabled; Prices for Helpers**: Free of charge for both the disabled & helpers
TOILETS : **Location of Disabled Toilets (+ Number)**: 2 toilets available
BLIND : **Facilities Available**: Commentaries Available (Please contact club for further information)
BOOKINGS : **Are Bookings Necessary**: Yes **CONTACT NUMBER**: (0272) 632812

BRISTOL ROVERS FC

WHEELCHAIRS : **Location of Accommodation**: Accommodated in front of Family Stand
Nº Spaces for Home Fans; Nº Spaces for Away Fans: 14 Spaces available in total
Are Helpers Admitted; Nº Admitted: One helper admitted per disabled supporter
PRICES : **Prices for Disabled; Prices for Helpers**: Free of charge for both the disabled & helpers
TOILETS : **Location of Disabled Toilets (+ Number)**: One available in Family Stand
BLIND : **Facilities Available**: Commentaries Available by Arrangement (please contact club early)
BOOKINGS : **Are Bookings Necessary**: Yes **CONTACT NUMBER**: (0272) 352508

BURNLEY FC

WHEELCHAIRS : **Location of Accommodation**: In Front of Bob Lord Stand
Nº Spaces for Home Fans; Nº Spaces for Away Fans: Limited Number of Spaces
Are Helpers Admitted; Nº Admitted: One helper admitted per disabled supporter
PRICES : **Prices for Disabled; Prices for Helpers**: Childrens prices for disabled. Full-price for helpers
TOILETS : **Location of Disabled Toilets (+ Number)**: None
BLIND : **Facilities Available**: Commentaries via headsets available
BOOKINGS : **Are Bookings Necessary**: Yes **CONTACT NUMBER**: (0282) 427777 (Mrs.P.Scott)

BURY FC

WHEELCHAIRS : **Location of Accommodation**: Accommodated in new area in South Stand.
Nº Spaces for Home Fans; Nº Spaces for Away Fans: Not Specified
Are Helpers Admitted; Nº Admitted: Helpers admitted - unspecified number
PRICES : **Prices for Disabled; Prices for Helpers**: Disabled half-price. Helpers full-price
TOILETS : **Location of Disabled Toilets (+ Number)**: Available in new disabled section (being built)
BLIND : **Facilities Available**: Radio Commentary in Press Box
BOOKINGS : **Are Bookings Necessary**: Yes **CONTACT NUMBER**: (061) 764-4881

CAMBRIDGE UNITED FC

WHEELCHAIRS : **Location of Accommodation**: In Disabled Section - in front of Main Stand
Nº Spaces for Home Fans; Nº Spaces for Away Fans: 12 Spaces available in total
Are Helpers Admitted; Nº Admitted: One helper admitted per disabled supporter
PRICES : **Prices for Disabled; Prices for Helpers**: Free of Charge for the disabled. Half-price for helpers
TOILETS : **Location of Disabled Toilets (+ Number)**: Available at rear of Disabled Enclosure
BLIND : **Facilities Available**: No Special Facilities
BOOKINGS : **Are Bookings Necessary**: Yes **CONTACT NUMBER**: (0223) 566500

Cardiff City FC

Wheelchairs : **Location of Accommodation**: Accommodated in Canton Stand/Popular Bank Corner
Nº Spaces for Home Fans; Nº Spaces for Away Fans: 20 spaces each for Home & Away
Are Helpers Admitted; Nº Admitted: One helper admitted per disabled supporter
Prices : **Prices for Disabled; Prices for Helpers**: Please phone for details
Toilets : **Location of Disabled Toilets (+ Number)**: None
Blind : **Facilities Available**: No Special Facilities
Bookings : **Are Bookings Necessary**: No **Contact Number**: (0222) 398636

Carlisle United FC

Wheelchairs : **Location of Accommodation**: Disabled Section (in front of paddock) by Prior Arrangement
Nº Spaces for Home Fans; Nº Spaces for Away Fans: Limited Number of Spaces
Are Helpers Admitted; Nº Admitted: One helper admitted per disabled supporter
Prices : **Prices for Disabled; Prices for Helpers**: Will advise when booking
Toilets : **Location of Disabled Toilets (+ Number)**: None
Blind : **Facilities Available**: Commentaries Available
Bookings : **Are Bookings Necessary**: Yes **Contact Number**: (0228) 26237

Charlton Athletic FC

Wheelchairs : **Location of Accommodation**: Accommodated in West Stand and East Stand
Nº Spaces for Home Fans; Nº Spaces for Away Fans: 40 spaces available in total
Are Helpers Admitted; Nº Admitted: Yes - up to 40 helpers are admitted
Prices : **Prices for Disabled; Prices for Helpers**: Free of charge
Toilets : **Location of Disabled Toilets (+ Number)**: Available in West Stand & East Stand
Blind : **Facilities Available**: Yes - please ring for details
Bookings : **Are Bookings Necessary**: Yes **Contact Number**: (081) 293-4567

Chelsea FC

Wheelchairs : **Location of Accommodation**: Accommodated in front of South Terrace
Nº Spaces for Home Fans; Nº Spaces for Away Fans: Approximately 40 spaces in total
Are Helpers Admitted; Nº Admitted: One helper admitted per disabled person
Prices : **Prices for Disabled; Prices for Helpers**: Free of charge for disabled. Full price for helpers
Toilets : **Location of Disabled Toilets (+ Number)**: East Stand Concourse: 1 male and 1 female
Blind : **Facilities Available**: No Special Facilities
Bookings : **Are Bookings Necessary**: Yes **Contact Number**: (071) 385-5545

Chester City FC

Wheelchairs : **Location of Accommodation**: West Stand & East Stand
Nº Spaces for Home Fans; Nº Spaces for Away Fans: 72 spaces available in total
Are Helpers Admitted; Nº Admitted: One helper admitted per disabled person
Prices : **Prices for Disabled; Prices for Helpers**: Free of charge for the disabled. Helpers normal prices
Toilets : **Location of Disabled Toilets (+ Number)**: Available in West Stand & East Stand
Blind : **Facilities Available**: No Special Facilities - But phone for further information
Bookings : **Are Bookings Necessary**: Yes **Contact Number**: (0244) 371376

Chesterfield FC

Wheelchairs : **Location of Accommodation**: Below Saltergate Wing Stand
Nº Spaces for Home Fans; Nº Spaces for Away Fans: 20 Spaces available in total
Are Helpers Admitted; Nº Admitted: One helper admitted per disabled supporter
Prices : **Prices for Disabled; Prices for Helpers**: Free of charge for the disabled. Helpers £6.50
Toilets : **Location of Disabled Toilets (+ Number)**: One available underneath Main Stand
Blind : **Facilities Available**: No Special Facilities
Bookings : **Are Bookings Necessary**: Yes **Contact Number**: (0246) 209765

Colchester United FC

Wheelchairs : **Location of Accommodation**: On Terrace next to Main Stand
Nº Spaces for Home Fans; Nº Spaces for Away Fans: 6 spaces available in total
Are Helpers Admitted; Nº Admitted: Yes
Prices : **Prices for Disabled; Prices for Helpers**: Free for the disabled. Helpers charged terrace prices
Toilets : **Location of Disabled Toilets (+ Number)**: Yes - Available under Main Stand
Blind : **Facilities Available**: Commentaries available for 3 people
Bookings : **Are Bookings Necessary**: Yes **Contact Number**: (0206) 574042

Coventry City FC

Wheelchairs : **Location of Accommodation**: Disabled Section in Clock Stand
Nº Spaces for Home Fans; Nº Spaces for Away Fans: 24 spaces in total
Are Helpers Admitted; Nº Admitted: Up to 47 helpers admitted
Prices : **Prices for Disabled; Prices for Helpers**: £4.00 for the disabled. £8.00 for helpers
Toilets : **Location of Disabled Toilets (+ Number)**: 2 - adjacent to disabled area
Blind : **Facilities Available**: Via Hospital Radio Commentary
Bookings : **Are Bookings Necessary**: Yes **Contact Number** (0203) 225545

Crewe Alexandra FC

Wheelchairs : **Location of Accommodation**: Family Stand
Nº Spaces for Home Fans; Nº Spaces for Away Fans: Approx. 7 spaces available in total
Are Helpers Admitted; Nº Admitted: One helper admitted per disabled supporter
Prices : **Prices for Disabled; Prices for Helpers**: £5.00 in total for each disabled supporter and helper
Toilets : **Location of Disabled Toilets (+ Number)**: Available in Family Stand
Blind : **Facilities Available**: Commentaries Available
Bookings : **Are Bookings Necessary**: Yes **Contact Number**: (0270) 213014

Crystal Palace FC

Wheelchairs : **Location of Accommodation**: In Disabled Section - Arthur Wait Stand (Park Road Entrance)
Nº Spaces for Home Fans; Nº Spaces for Away Fans: 24 spaces for home fans; 4 for away
Are Helpers Admitted; Nº Admitted: One helper admitted per wheelchair
Prices : **Prices for Disabled; Prices for Helpers**: Disabled Free of Charge . Helpers pay full-price.
Toilets : **Location of Disabled Toilets (+ Number)**: Located in disabled section
Blind : **Facilities Available**: Commentaries Available - 6 places available
Bookings : **Are Bookings Necessary**: Yes **Contact Number**: (081) 653-4462

Darlington FC

Wheelchairs : **Location of Accommodation**: Accommodated in Disabled Section - East Stand
Nº Spaces for Home Fans; Nº Spaces for Away Fans: 20 spaces each for home & away fans
Are Helpers Admitted; Nº Admitted: One helper admitted with each disabled person
Prices : **Prices for Disabled; Prices for Helpers**: No concessions - full price.
Toilets : **Location of Disabled Toilets (+ Number)**: None
Blind : **Facilities Available**: No Special Facilities
Bookings : **Are Bookings Necessary**: No **Contact Number**: (0325) 465097

Derby County FC

Wheelchairs : **Location of Accommodation**: Accommodated in Disabled Section - Normanton End
Nº Spaces for Home Fans; Nº Spaces for Away Fans: 80 spaces available in total
Are Helpers Admitted; Nº Admitted: One helper admitted per disabled person
Prices : **Prices for Disabled; Prices for Helpers**: Free of charge for both the disabled and helpers
Toilets : **Location of Disabled Toilets (+ Number)**: Available in Disabled Section
Blind : **Facilities Available**: Commentaries available in Disabled Viewing Gallery
Bookings : **Are Bookings Necessary**: Yes **Contact Number**: (0332) 340105

Doncaster Rovers FC

Wheelchairs : **Location of Accommodation**: Accommodated in Disabled Section - 'A' Block
Nº Spaces for Home Fans; Nº Spaces for Away Fans: Limited number of spaces available
Are Helpers Admitted; Nº Admitted: One helper admitted per wheelchair
Prices : **Prices for Disabled; Prices for Helpers**: Free of charge for both the disabled & the helpers
Toilets : **Location of Disabled Toilets (+ Number)**: None
Blind : **Facilities Available**: No Special Facilities
Bookings : **Are Bookings Necessary**: Yes **Contact Number**: (0302) 539441

Everton FC

Wheelchairs : **Location of Accommodation**: Disabled Section - Bullens Road
Nº Spaces for Home Fans; Nº Spaces for Away Fans: 25 spaces for home fans; 5 for away
Are Helpers Admitted; Nº Admitted: One helper admitted with each wheelchair
Prices : **Prices for Disabled; Prices for Helpers**: Free for the disabled. £8.50 - £13.00 for helpers
Toilets : **Location of Disabled Toilets (+ Number)**: One in Disabled Section
Blind : **Facilities Available**: Seats with commentaries available
Bookings : **Are Bookings Necessary**: Yes **Contact Number**: (051) 521-2020

EXETER CITY FC

WHEELCHAIRS : **Location of Accommodation**: In front of Main Grandstand
Nº Spaces for Home Fans; Nº Spaces for Away Fans: Limited Number
Are Helpers Admitted; Nº Admitted: One helper admitted per wheelchair
PRICES : **Prices for Disabled; Prices for Helpers**: Free of charge for the disabled. £8.00 per helper
TOILETS : **Location of Disabled Toilets (+ Number)**: None
BLIND : **Facilities Available**: No Special Facilities
BOOKINGS : **Are Bookings Necessary**: Yes **CONTACT NUMBER**: (0392) 54073

FULHAM FC

WHEELCHAIRS : **Location of Accommodation**: Disabled Section - alongside Miller Stand Touchline
Nº Spaces for Home Fans; Nº Spaces for Away Fans: 20 spaces in total
Are Helpers Admitted; Nº Admitted: One helper admitted per disabled person
PRICES : **Prices for Disabled; Prices for Helpers**: Free for the disabled. Helpers £6.50 (1994/95 prices)
TOILETS : **Location of Disabled Toilets (+ Number)**: Available by Forecourt - Opposite Cottage
BLIND : **Facilities Available**: Commentaries Available by Prior Arrangement
BOOKINGS : **Are Bookings Necessary**: Yes **CONTACT NUMBER**: (071) 736-6561

GILLINGHAM FC

WHEELCHAIRS : **Location of Accommodation**: Disabled Section - adjacent to Main Stand (Redfern Avenue)
Nº Spaces for Home Fans; Nº Spaces for Away Fans: 20 spaces available in total
Are Helpers Admitted; Nº Admitted: One helper admitted per disabled supporter
PRICES : **Prices for Disabled; Prices for Helpers**: Both helpers and disabled pay normal ground prices
TOILETS : **Location of Disabled Toilets (+ Number)**: None
BLIND : **Facilities Available**: No Special Facilities
BOOKINGS : **Are Bookings Necessary**: Preferred **CONTACT NUMBER**: (0634) 851462

GRIMSBY TOWN FC

WHEELCHAIRS : **Location of Accommodation**: Accommodated in Disabled Section - Main Stand
Nº Spaces for Home Fans; Nº Spaces for Away Fans: 50 spaces available in total
Are Helpers Admitted; Nº Admitted: Yes
PRICES : **Prices for Disabled; Prices for Helpers**: Disabled free of charge, helpers normal prices
TOILETS : **Location of Disabled Toilets (+ Number)**: In Disabled Section
BLIND : **Facilities Available**: Commentaries Available in Disabled Section
BOOKINGS : **Are Bookings Necessary**: No **CONTACT NUMBER**: (0472) 697111

HARTLEPOOL UNITED FC

WHEELCHAIRS : **Location of Accommodation**: Disabled Section - Mill House side of Ground
Nº Spaces for Home Fans; Nº Spaces for Away Fans: Total of 20 spaces available
Are Helpers Admitted; Nº Admitted: One helper admitted with each disabled supporter
PRICES : **Prices for Disabled; Prices for Helpers**: £4.00 for the disabled. £6.00 for helpers
TOILETS : **Location of Disabled Toilets (+ Number)**: None
BLIND : **Facilities Available**: Commentaries Available
BOOKINGS : **Are Bookings Necessary**: No **CONTACT NUMBER**: (0429) 272584

HEREFORD UNITED FC

WHEELCHAIRS : **Location of Accommodation**: Accommodated in Disabled Section - Edgar Street Side
Nº Spaces for Home Fans; Nº Spaces for Away Fans: 10 spaces in total
Are Helpers Admitted; Nº Admitted: One helper admitted per disabled supporter
PRICES : **Prices for Disabled; Prices for Helpers**: £4.00 each for both the disabled and helpers
TOILETS : **Location of Disabled Toilets (+ Number)**: None
BLIND : **Facilities Available**: No Special Facilities
BOOKINGS : **Are Bookings Necessary**: No **CONTACT NUMBER**: (0432) 276666

HUDDERSFIELD TOWN FC

WHEELCHAIRS : **Location of Accommodation**: Disabled Sections - Riverside Stand, Kilner Bank Stand
Nº Spaces for Home Fans; Nº Spaces for Away Fans: 169 spaces available in total
Are Helpers Admitted; Nº Admitted: One helper admitted per wheelchair
PRICES : **Prices for Disabled; Prices for Helpers**: Concessionary rates for both disabled and helpers
TOILETS : **Location of Disabled Toilets (+ Number)**: Available in disabled sections
BLIND : **Facilities Available**: Commentaries available
BOOKINGS : **Are Bookings Necessary**: No **CONTACT NUMBER**: (0484) 420335

Hull City FC

Wheelchairs : **Location of Accommodation**: Accommodated in Disabled Enclosure - South East Corner
Nº Spaces for Home Fans; Nº Spaces for Away Fans: Approximately 20 spaces in total
Are Helpers Admitted; Nº Admitted: One helper admitted per disabled person
Prices : **Prices for Disabled; Prices for Helpers**: Free of charge for the disabled. £6.00 per helper
Toilets : **Location of Disabled Toilets (+ Number)**: One toilet situated within disabled enclosure
Blind : **Facilities Available**: Commentaries Available
Bookings : **Are Bookings Necessary**: No **Contact Number**: (0482) 51119

Ipswich Town FC

Wheelchairs : **Location of Accommodation**: Disabled Section - Pioneer Stand; Away - Portman Stand
Nº Spaces for Home Fans; Away Fans: 30 spaces + 50 seats home; 6 spaces + 14 seats away
Are Helpers Admitted; Nº Admitted: One helper admitted per disabled person
Prices : **Prices for Disabled; Prices for Helpers**: Free of charge for the disabled. £8.50 for helpers
Toilets : **Location of Disabled Toilets (+ Number)**: Adjacent to Stand
Blind : **Facilities Available**: Commentaries Available
Bookings : **Are Bookings Necessary**: Yes **Contact Number**: (0473) 219211

Leeds United FC

Wheelchairs : **Location of Accommodation**: Accommodated in Disabled Section - West Stand & S.W.Corner
Nº Spaces for Home Fans; Nº Spaces for Away Fans: 80 spaces for wheelchairs in total
Are Helpers Admitted; Nº Admitted: One helper admitted per disabled person
Prices : **Prices for Disabled; Prices for Helpers**: Free of charge for the disabled. £12.00 for helpers
Toilets : **Location of Disabled Toilets (+ Number)**: One adjacent to each of the Disabled Sections
Blind : **Facilities Available**: Commentaries via Headphones in West Stand
Bookings : **Are Bookings Necessary**: Yes **Contact Number**: (0532) 716037

Leicester City FC

Wheelchairs : **Location of Accommodation**: Accommodated in Carling Stand Lower Tier
Nº Spaces for Home Fans; Nº Spaces for Away Fans: Over 30 spaces available
Are Helpers Admitted; Nº Admitted: One helper admitted per disabled person
Prices : **Prices for Disabled; Prices for Helpers**: Free of charge for the disabled. £8.00 for helpers
Toilets : **Location of Disabled Toilets (+ Number)**: Available in Carling Stand
Blind : **Facilities Available**: No Special Facilities at present
Bookings : **Are Bookings Necessary**: Yes **Contact Number**: (0533) 555000

Leyton Orient FC

Wheelchairs : **Location of Accommodation**: Accommodated in Disabled Section - North Terrace
Nº Spaces for Home Fans; Nº Spaces for Away Fans: 12 spaces available in total
Are Helpers Admitted; Nº Admitted: One helper admitted per disabled supporter
Prices : **Prices for Disabled; Prices for Helpers**: Free of charge for both the disabled and helpers
Toilets : **Location of Disabled Toilets (+ Number)**: One available near Disabled Section
Blind : **Facilities Available**: Commentary - contact Football in the Community (081) 556-5973
Bookings : **Are Bookings Necessary**: Yes **Contact Number**: (081) 539-2223

Lincoln City FC

Wheelchairs : **Location of Accommodation**: Accommodated - Adjacent to Turnstile 1
Nº Spaces for Home Fans; Nº Spaces for Away Fans: 62 spaces available in total
Are Helpers Admitted; Nº Admitted: One helper admitted per disabled supporter
Prices : **Prices for Disabled; Prices for Helpers**: Free of charge for the disabled. Full-price for Helpers.
Toilets : **Location of Disabled Toilets (+ Number)**: Several adjacent to disabled accommodation
Blind : **Facilities Available**: No Special facilities
Bookings : **Are Bookings Necessary**: Yes **Contact Number**: (0522) 522224

Liverpool FC

Wheelchairs : **Location of Accommodation**: Paddock Enclosure (more spaces when Kop Stand completed)
Nº Spaces for Home Fans; Nº Spaces for Away Fans: 17 spaces for home. None for away.
Are Helpers Admitted; Nº Admitted: Up to 30 helpers are admitted
Prices : **Prices for Disabled; Prices for Helpers**: £3.00 per disabled person. £13 or £14 per helper
Toilets : **Location of Disabled Toilets (+ Number)**: One in the Paddock
Blind : **Facilities Available**: Commentaries Available in Disabled Section
Bookings : **Are Bookings Necessary**: Yes **Contact Number**: (051) 260-8680

LUTON TOWN FC

WHEELCHAIRS : **Location of Accommodation**: In Main Stand
Nº Spaces for Home Fans; Nº Spaces for Away Fans: 15 spaces available in total
Are Helpers Admitted; Nº Admitted: One helper admitted per disabled person
PRICES : **Prices for Disabled; Prices for Helpers**: Free of charge for both disabled and helpers
TOILETS : **Location of Disabled Toilets (+ Number)**: One adjacent to the disabled area
BLIND : **Facilities Available**: Commentaries Available
BOOKINGS : **Are Bookings Necessary**: Yes **CONTACT NUMBER**: (0582) 411622

MANCHESTER CITY FC

WHEELCHAIRS : **Location of Accommodation**: Umbro Stand
Nº Spaces for Home Fans; Nº Spaces for Away Fans: 56 spaces available in total
Are Helpers Admitted; Nº Admitted: One helper admitted per wheelchair
PRICES : **Prices for Disabled; Prices for Helpers**: Disabled - free of charge. Helpers £4.00
TOILETS : **Location of Disabled Toilets (+ Number)**: 7 Available within Umbro Stand
BLIND : **Facilities Available**: Hospital Commentaries for 11 blind + helpers - Main Stand, G Block
BOOKINGS : **Are Bookings Necessary**: Yes **CONTACT NUMBER**: (061) 226-1191

MANCHESTER UNITED FC

WHEELCHAIRS : **Location of Accommodation**: Disabled Section - In front of 'L' Stand
Nº Spaces for Home Fans; Nº Spaces for Away Fans: 32 spaces available in total
Are Helpers Admitted; Nº Admitted: One helper admitted per disabled fan
PRICES : **Prices for Disabled; Prices for Helpers**: Free of Charge for both disabled & helpers
TOILETS : **Location of Disabled Toilets (+ Number)**: Located near Disabled Section
BLIND : **Facilities Available**: Commentaries Available
BOOKINGS : **Are Bookings Necessary**: Yes **CONTACT NUMBER**: (061) 872-1661

MANSFIELD TOWN FC

WHEELCHAIRS : **Location of Accommodation**: Accommodated - North End of Bishop Street Terrace (covered)
Nº Spaces for Home Fans; Nº Spaces for Away Fans: 40 spaces available in total
Are Helpers Admitted; Nº Admitted: Yes
PRICES : **Prices for Disabled; Prices for Helpers**: Free of charge for the disabled. Helpers full-price
TOILETS : **Location of Disabled Toilets (+ Number)**: Adjacent to terrace
BLIND : **Facilities Available**: No Special Facilities
BOOKINGS : **Are Bookings Necessary**: Not Usually **CONTACT NUMBER**: (0623) 23567

MIDDLESBROUGH FC

WHEELCHAIRS : **Location of Accommodation**: Accommodated in North East Corner
Nº Spaces for Home Fans; Nº Spaces for Away Fans: 20 spaces available in total
Are Helpers Admitted; Nº Admitted: One helper admitted per disabled person
PRICES : **Prices for Disabled; Prices for Helpers**: £3.00 per disabled person, £6.00 per helper
TOILETS : **Location of Disabled Toilets (+ Number)**: One available in North East Corner
BLIND : **Facilities Available**: Commentaries Available - 40 headsets
BOOKINGS : **Are Bookings Necessary**: Yes **CONTACT NUMBER**: (0642) 826664

MILLWALL FC

WHEELCHAIRS : **Location of Accommodation**: Accommodated in Disabled Section - West Stand
Nº Spaces for Home Fans; Nº Spaces for Away Fans: 200 spaces available in total
Are Helpers Admitted; Nº Admitted: One helper admitted per disabled person
PRICES : **Prices for Disabled; Prices for Helpers**: Free of charge for the disabled. Helpers £10.00
TOILETS : **Location of Disabled Toilets (+ Number)**: 17 toilets available around the Stadium
BLIND : **Facilities Available**: Commentaries available
BOOKINGS : **Are Bookings Necessary**: Yes **CONTACT NUMBER**: (071) 232-1222

NEWCASTLE UNITED FC

WHEELCHAIRS : **Location of Accommodation**: Available in Disabled Areas - Sir John Hall Stand & South Stand
Nº Spaces for Home Fans; Nº Spaces for Away Fans: 74 spaces available in total
Are Helpers Admitted; Nº Admitted: One helper admitted per disabled supporter
PRICES : **Prices for Disabled; Prices for Helpers**: Prices on application
TOILETS : **Location of Disabled Toilets (+ Number)**: Available in Sir John Hall Stand
BLIND : **Facilities Available**: Facilities for 20 blind supporters with Match Commentaries
BOOKINGS : **Are Bookings Necessary**: Yes **CONTACT NUMBER**: (091) 232-8361

Northampton Town FC

Wheelchairs : **Location of Accommodation**: Various locations of disabled areas around the ground
Nº Spaces for Home Fans; Nº Spaces for Away Fans: Over 30 spaces available in total
Are Helpers Admitted; Nº Admitted: One helper admitted per disabled supporter
Prices : **Prices for Disabled; Prices for Helpers**: Free of charge for the disabled. Helpers full-price
Toilets : **Location of Disabled Toilets (+ Number)**: Available by Disabled Areas
Blind : **Facilities Available**: No Special Facilities
Bookings : **Are Bookings Necessary**: Yes **Contact Number**: (0604) 234100

Norwich City FC

Wheelchairs : **Location of Accommodation**: South Stand/River End corner (Glazed & Heated)
Nº Spaces for Home Fans; Nº Spaces for Away Fans: 34 spaces for home fans; 6 for away
Are Helpers Admitted; Nº Admitted: One helper admitted for each disabled person
Prices : **Prices for Disabled; Prices for Helpers**: Free of charge for both the disabled and helpers
Toilets : **Location of Disabled Toilets (+ Number)**: One within disabled enclosure
Blind : **Facilities Available**: No Special Facilities
Bookings : **Are Bookings Necessary**: Yes **Contact Number**: (0603) 761661

Nottingham Forest FC

Wheelchairs : **Location of Accommodation**: Disabled Section - In front of Executive Stand
Nº Spaces for Home Fans; Nº Spaces for Away Fans: 50 spaces available in total
Are Helpers Admitted; Nº Admitted: One helper admitted per disabled supporter
Prices : **Prices for Disabled; Prices for Helpers**: Free of charge for the disabled. £12.00 for helpers
Toilets : **Location of Disabled Toilets (+ Number)**: Available in Executive Stand
Blind : **Facilities Available**: No Special Facilities
Bookings : **Are Bookings Necessary**: Yes **Contact Number**: (0602) 813801

Notts County FC

Wheelchairs : **Location of Accommodation**: Disabled Section - County Road/Meadow Lane End Corner
Nº Spaces for Home Fans; Nº Spaces for Away Fans: 100 spaces in total
Are Helpers Admitted; Nº Admitted: One helper admitted per disabled supporter
Prices : **Prices for Disabled; Prices for Helpers**: Free of charge for the disabled. Helpers full price
Toilets : **Location of Disabled Toilets (+ Number)**: Next to disabled area
Blind : **Facilities Available**: No Special Facilities
Bookings : **Are Bookings Necessary**: Yes **Contact Number**: (0602) 861155/850632

Oldham Athletic FC

Wheelchairs : **Location of Accommodation**: Lookers Paddock, Seton Stand & Rochdale Road Stand
Nº Spaces for Home Fans; Nº Spaces for Away Fans: 36 spaces available in total
Are Helpers Admitted; Nº Admitted: One helper admitted per disabled supporter
Prices : **Prices for Disabled; Prices for Helpers**: Free of charge for the disabled. Full-prices for helpers
Toilets : **Location of Disabled Toilets (+ Number)**: In Lookers Paddock & Rochdale Road Stand
Blind : **Facilities Available**: Commentaries Available
Bookings : **Are Bookings Necessary**: Yes **Contact Number**: (061) 624-4972

Oxford United FC

Wheelchairs : **Location of Accommodation**: Disabled Section - Beech Road Corner
Nº Spaces for Home Fans; Nº Spaces for Away Fans: 25 spaces available in total
Are Helpers Admitted; Nº Admitted: One helper admitted per disabled person (25 max.)
Prices : **Prices for Disabled; Prices for Helpers**: £5.00 for the disabled. Helpers normal prices
Toilets : **Location of Disabled Toilets (+ Number)**: One available in Beech Road Corner
Blind : **Facilities Available**: No Special Facilities
Bookings : **Are Bookings Necessary**: Yes **Contact Number**: (0865) 61503

Peterborough United FC

Wheelchairs : **Location of Accommodation**: Accommodated in Disabled Area - Right Side of Main Stand
Nº Spaces for Home Fans; Nº Spaces for Away Fans: 12 spaces available in total
Are Helpers Admitted; Nº Admitted: One helper admitted per disabled supporter
Prices : **Prices for Disabled; Prices for Helpers**: £5.00 for the disabled and helpers (1992/93 prices)
Toilets : **Location of Disabled Toilets (+ Number)**: None
Blind : **Facilities Available**: No Special Facilities
Bookings : **Are Bookings Necessary**: Yes **Contact Number**: (0733) 63947

Plymouth Argyle FC

Wheelchairs : **Location of Accommodation**: Accommodated in Disabled Section in Devonport End
Nº Spaces for Home Fans; Nº Spaces for Away Fans: Total of 60 spaces available
Are Helpers Admitted; Nº Admitted: One helper admitted per disabled person
Prices : **Prices for Disabled; Prices for Helpers**: Free of charge for the disabled. £5.50 for helpers
Toilets : **Location of Disabled Toilets (+ Number)**: Adjacent to disabled section
Blind : **Facilities Available**: Commentaries Available
Bookings : **Are Bookings Necessary**: Yes **Contact Number**: (0752) 562561

Portsmouth FC

Wheelchairs : **Location of Accommodation**: Accommodated in Disabled Section - Fratton Road End
Nº Spaces for Home Fans; Nº Spaces for Away Fans: Limited number of spaces available
Are Helpers Admitted; Nº Admitted: One helper admitted per disabled supporter
Prices : **Prices for Disabled; Prices for Helpers**: Free of charge for both the disabled and helpers
Toilets : **Location of Disabled Toilets (+ Number)**: One in disabled section
Blind : **Facilities Available**: No Special Facilities
Bookings : **Are Bookings Necessary**: Yes **Contact Number**: (0705) 731204

Port Vale FC

Wheelchairs : **Location of Accommodation**: Disabled Section - Lorne Street/Hamil Road Corner
Nº Spaces for Home Fans; Nº Spaces for Away Fans: 72 spaces available in total
Are Helpers Admitted; Nº Admitted: One helper admitted per disabled person on request
Prices : **Prices for Disabled; Prices for Helpers**: £3.50 for the disabled, £6.50 for helpers
Toilets : **Location of Disabled Toilets (+ Number)**: One available in Disabled Section
Blind : **Facilities Available**: Commentaries are available - Please contact Club
Bookings : **Are Bookings Necessary**: Yes **Contact Number**: (0782) 814134

Preston North End FC

Wheelchairs : **Location of Accommodation**: Perimeter track in front of West Stand Paddocks (Deepdale Rd.)
Nº Spaces for Home Fans; Nº Spaces for Away Fans: 20 spaces available in total
Are Helpers Admitted; Nº Admitted: Usually one helper per wheelchair. More if necessary.
Prices : **Prices for Disabled; Prices for Helpers**: Disabled plus one helper free. Others full price
Toilets : **Location of Disabled Toilets (+ Number)**: One available at Invalid Entrance - Deepdale Road
Blind : **Facilities Available**: Commentaries available
Bookings : **Are Bookings Necessary**: Sometimes **Contact Number**: (0772) 795919

Queens Park Rangers FC

Wheelchairs : **Location of Accommodation**: In Wheelchair enclosure - Left Side of Ellerslie Road Stand
Nº Spaces for Home Fans; Nº Spaces for Away Fans: Total of 18 spaces available.
Are Helpers Admitted; Nº Admitted: One helper admitted per wheelchair
Prices : **Prices for Disabled; Prices for Helpers**: Free of charge for both the disabled and helpers
Toilets : **Location of Disabled Toilets (+ Number)**: Available in Corner of Ellerslie Road Stand
Blind : **Facilities Available**: No Special Facilities
Bookings : **Are Bookings Necessary**: Yes **Contact Number**: Please contact in writing

Reading FC

Wheelchairs : **Location of Accommodation**: Accommodated in Front Row 'E' Stand
Nº Spaces for Home Fans; Nº Spaces for Away Fans: 15 spaces available in total
Are Helpers Admitted; Nº Admitted: Yes
Prices : **Prices for Disabled; Prices for Helpers**: Free of charge for the disabled and helpers
Toilets : **Location of Disabled Toilets (+ Number)**: One adjacent to stand
Blind : **Facilities Available**: No Special Facilities
Bookings : **Are Bookings Necessary**: Yes **Contact Number**: (0734) 507878

Rochdale FC

Wheelchairs : **Location of Accommodation**: Main Stand
Nº Spaces for Home Fans; Nº Spaces for Away Fans: 12 spaces available in total
Are Helpers Admitted; Nº Admitted: One helper admitted per disabled person
Prices : **Prices for Disabled; Prices for Helpers**: Free of charge for the disabled. £5.00 per helper
Toilets : **Location of Disabled Toilets (+ Number)**: Adjacent to Disabled Area
Blind : **Facilities Available**: No Special Facilities
Bookings : **Are Bookings Necessary**: Yes **Contact Number**: (0706) 44648

Rotherham United FC

Wheelchairs : **Location of Accommodation**: Accommodated in Disabled Section - Millmoor Lane
Nº Spaces for Home Fans; Nº Spaces for Away Fans: 7 spaces available
Are Helpers Admitted; Nº Admitted: One helper admitted per disabled person
Prices : **Prices for Disabled; Prices for Helpers**: Free of charge for both the disabled and helpers
Toilets : **Location of Disabled Toilets (+ Number)**: None
Blind : **Facilities Available**: No Special Facilities
Bookings : **Are Bookings Necessary**: Yes **Contact Number**: (0709) 562434

Scarborough FC

Wheelchairs : **Location of Accommodation**: Adjacent to Main Stand
Nº Spaces for Home Fans; Nº Spaces for Away Fans: 10 spaces available in total
Are Helpers Admitted; Nº Admitted: One helper admitted per wheelchair
Prices : **Prices for Disabled; Prices for Helpers**: Full-price for both the disabled and helpers
Toilets : **Location of Disabled Toilets (+ Number)**: Available at rear of Disabled Area
Blind : **Facilities Available**: No Special Facilities
Bookings : **Are Bookings Necessary**: Yes **Contact Number**: (0723) 375094

Scunthorpe United FC

Wheelchairs : **Location of Accommodation**: Accommodated in Disabled Section - Clugston Stand
Nº Spaces for Home Fans; Nº Spaces for Away Fans: 12 spaces each for home & away fans
Are Helpers Admitted; Nº Admitted: One helper admitted per disabled fan
Prices : **Prices for Disabled; Prices for Helpers**: Free of charge for the disabled. Full-price for helpers
Toilets : **Location of Disabled Toilets (+ Number)**: One in the Clugston Stand
Blind : **Facilities Available**: Commentaries Available
Bookings : **Are Bookings Necessary**: Yes **Contact Number**: (0724) 848077

Sheffield United FC

Wheelchairs : **Location of Accommodation**: Accommodated in Disabled Section - Members Area
Nº Spaces for Home Fans; Nº Spaces for Away Fans: Limited for number available
Are Helpers Admitted; Nº Admitted: One helper admitted per wheelchair
Prices : **Prices for Disabled; Prices for Helpers**: Free of charge for both the disabled and helpers
Toilets : **Location of Disabled Toilets (+ Number)**: 3 available within the enclosure
Blind : **Facilities Available**: Commentaries Available on Request
Bookings : **Are Bookings Necessary**: Yes **Contact Number**: (0742) 738955

Sheffield Wednesday FC

Wheelchairs : **Location of Accommodation**: Accommodated in Disabled Section - North Stand
Nº Spaces for Home Fans; Nº Spaces for Away Fans: Number not specified
Are Helpers Admitted; Nº Admitted: One helper admitted per disabled supporter
Prices : **Prices for Disabled; Prices for Helpers**: Normal Prices for both the disabled and helpers
Toilets : **Location of Disabled Toilets (+ Number)**: Available within the North Stand
Blind : **Facilities Available**: Commentaries Available
Bookings : **Are Bookings Necessary**: Yes **Contact Number**: (0742) 343122

Shrewsbury Town FC

Wheelchairs : **Location of Accommodation**: No specific area, but along pitchside if necessary
Nº Spaces for Home Fans; Nº Spaces for Away Fans: No fixed numbers
Are Helpers Admitted; Nº Admitted: One helper per disabled supporter
Prices : **Prices for Disabled; Prices for Helpers**: Free of charge for the disabled. Full-price for helpers
Toilets : **Location of Disabled Toilets (+ Number)**: One available in Wakeman Stand
Blind : **Facilities Available**: No Special Facilities but can be accommodated
Bookings : **Are Bookings Necessary**: Yes **Contact Number**: (0743) 360111

Southampton FC

Wheelchairs : **Location of Accommodation**: Limited Accommodation - Under West Stand
Nº Spaces for Home Fans; Nº Spaces for Away Fans: 10 spaces available in total
Are Helpers Admitted; Nº Admitted: One helper admitted per disabled person
Prices : **Prices for Disabled; Prices for Helpers**: Free of charge for the disabled. Helpers £9.00/£10.00
Toilets : **Location of Disabled Toilets (+ Number)**: By disabled entrance
Blind : **Facilities Available**: Commentaries Available
Bookings : **Are Bookings Necessary**: Yes **Contact Number**: (0703) 667547 Mr.Mortimer

Southend United FC

Wheelchairs : **Location of Accommodation**: Accommodated in Disabled Section - West Stand
Nº Spaces for Home Fans; Nº Spaces for Away Fans: 20 spaces available in total
Are Helpers Admitted; Nº Admitted: One helper admitted per disabled person
Prices : **Prices for Disabled; Prices for Helpers**: £4.50 per wheelchair. £9 per adult helper
Toilets : **Location of Disabled Toilets (+ Number)**: One available in disabled area
Blind : **Facilities Available**: Commentaries Available
Bookings : **Are Bookings Necessary**: Yes **Contact Number**: (0702) 435602

Stockport County FC

Wheelchairs : **Location of Accommodation**: Accommodated in Disabled Section
Nº Spaces for Home Fans; Nº Spaces for Away Fans: Spaces available for 10 wheelchairs
Are Helpers Admitted; Nº Admitted: One helper admitted per disabled supporter
Prices : **Prices for Disabled; Prices for Helpers**: Free of charge for the disabled. Full-price for helpers
Toilets : **Location of Disabled Toilets (+ Number)**: None
Blind : **Facilities Available**: None
Bookings : **Are Bookings Necessary**: Yes **Contact Number**: (061) 480-8888

Stoke City FC

Wheelchairs : **Location of Accommodation**: In Disabled Section - Corner Butler Street/Boothen End
Nº Spaces for Home Fans; Nº Spaces for Away Fans: 25 spaces available in total
Are Helpers Admitted; Nº Admitted: One helper admitted per disabled person
Prices : **Prices for Disabled; Prices for Helpers**: Free for disabled. Helpers £7 adult, Concession £5
Toilets : **Location of Disabled Toilets (+ Number)**: None
Blind : **Facilities Available**: 15 places available - Phone First
Bookings : **Are Bookings Necessary**: Yes **Contact Number**: (0782) 413511

Sunderland AFC

Wheelchairs : **Location of Accommodation**: Accommodated in Disabled Section - Roker End
Nº Spaces for Home Fans; Nº Spaces for Away Fans: 22 spaces for home fans; 1 for away
Are Helpers Admitted; Nº Admitted: One helper admitted per disabled person
Prices : **Prices for Disabled; Prices for Helpers**: Free of charge for both the disabled and helpers
Toilets : **Location of Disabled Toilets (+ Number)**: Toilets available in Roker End & Fulwell End
Blind : **Facilities Available**: Headphone Commentaries Available in Disabled Section (Main Stand)
Bookings : **Are Bookings Necessary**: Yes **Contact Number**: (091) 514-0332

Swansea City FC

Wheelchairs : **Location of Accommodation**: Accommodated - Centre Stand Touchline
Nº Spaces for Home Fans; Nº Spaces for Away Fans: Approximately 10 spaces available
Are Helpers Admitted; Nº Admitted: One helper admitted per wheelchair
Prices : **Prices for Disabled; Prices for Helpers**: Free of Charge for both the disabled and helpers
Toilets : **Location of Disabled Toilets (+ Number)**: None
Blind : **Facilities Available**: No Special Facilities
Bookings : **Are Bookings Necessary**: Yes **Contact Number**: (0792) 474114

Swindon Town FC

Wheelchairs : **Location of Accommodation**: Accommodated in Disabled Section - Town End Stand
Nº Spaces for Home Fans; Nº Spaces for Away Fans: 40 spaces available in total
Are Helpers Admitted; Nº Admitted: One helper admitted per disabled supporter
Prices : **Prices for Disabled; Prices for Helpers**: Free of charge for both the disabled and helpers
Toilets : **Location of Disabled Toilets (+ Number)**: One available within the Enclosure
Blind : **Facilities Available**: Commentaries Available in Disabled Section
Bookings : **Are Bookings Necessary**: Yes **Contact Number**: (0793) 430430

Torquay United FC

Wheelchairs : **Location of Accommodation**: Accommodated in front of the Ellacombe End Stand
Nº Spaces for Home Fans; Nº Spaces for Away Fans: Approximately 30 spaces available
Are Helpers Admitted; Nº Admitted: One helper admitted per disabled supporter
Prices : **Prices for Disabled; Prices for Helpers**: Free of charge for both the disabled and helpers
Toilets : **Location of Disabled Toilets (+ Number)**: 2 toilets available in Main Stand (one either end)
Blind : **Facilities Available**: Audio Facilities Available
Bookings : **Are Bookings Necessary**: Yes **Contact Number**: (0803) 328666

Tottenham Hotspur FC

Wheelchairs : **Location of Accommodation**: Home Support - North Stand Lower Tier; Away - South Stand
Nº Spaces for Home Fans; Nº Spaces for Away Fans: Home - 27 spaces; Away - 12 spaces
Are Helpers Admitted; Nº Admitted: One helper admitted per disabled person
Prices : **Prices for Disabled; Prices for Helpers**: Price for one disabled supporter + helper - £10.00
Toilets : **Location of Disabled Toilets (+ Number)**: 2 in Paxton Road enclosure, 1 near Park Lane
Blind : **Facilities Available**: No Special Facilities
Bookings : **Are Bookings Necessary**: Yes **Contact Number**: (081) 365-5000 ext. 5271

Tranmere Rovers FC

Wheelchairs : **Location of Accommodation**: Accommodated in Disabled Section - Family Enclosure
Nº Spaces for Home Fans; Nº Spaces for Away Fans: 25 spaces available in total
Are Helpers Admitted; Nº Admitted: One helper admitted per disabled supporter
Prices : **Prices for Disabled; Prices for Helpers**: Free of charge for the disabled. Helpers £6.00
Toilets : **Location of Disabled Toilets (+ Number)**: In Disabled Section - 2 available
Blind : **Facilities Available**: No Special Facilities
Bookings : **Are Bookings Necessary**: Yes **Contact Number**: (051) 608-0371

Walsall FC

Wheelchairs : **Location of Accommodation**: Accommodated in Highgate Stand
Nº Spaces for Home Fans; Nº Spaces for Away Fans: Total of 30 spaces available
Are Helpers Admitted; Nº Admitted: One adult helper admitted per disabled person
Prices : **Prices for Disabled; Prices for Helpers**: Free of charge for both disabled and helper
Toilets : **Location of Disabled Toilets (+ Number)**: Adjacent to disabled viewing bays
Blind : **Facilities Available**: Commentaries Planned
Bookings : **Are Bookings Necessary**: Yes **Contact Number**: (0922) 22791

Watford FC

Wheelchairs : **Location of Accommodation**: Accommodated in 2 Disabled Sections - S.E. Corner & North
Nº Spaces for Home Fans; Nº Spaces for Away Fans: Approximately 40 spaces in total
Are Helpers Admitted; Nº Admitted: One helper admitted per disabled person
Prices : **Prices for Disabled; Prices for Helpers**: £5.00 Adult for both disabled and helpers
Toilets : **Location of Disabled Toilets (+ Number)**: Adjacent to Enclosures
Blind : **Facilities Available**: Commentaries Available in East Stand - Free of charge
Bookings : **Are Bookings Necessary**: No **Contact Number**: (0923) 220393

West Bromwich Albion FC

Wheelchairs : **Location of Accommodation**: Accommodated - Birmingham Road End & Smethwick End
Nº Spaces for Home Fans; Nº Spaces for Away Fans: Approximately 30 spaces in total
Are Helpers Admitted; Nº Admitted: One helper admitted per disabled person
Prices : **Prices for Disabled; Prices for Helpers**: Free of charge for the disabled. £5.00 for helpers
Toilets : **Location of Disabled Toilets (+ Number)**: One available within the disabled section
Blind : **Facilities Available**: Accommodation for six listeners and six guides
Bookings : **Are Bookings Necessary**: Yes **Contact Number**: (021) 525-8888

West Ham United FC

Wheelchairs : **Location of Accommodation**: Limited Accommodation in Disabled Area - West Stand
Nº Spaces for Home Fans; Nº Spaces for Away Fans: 16 spaces for home fans, 4 for away
Are Helpers Admitted; Nº Admitted: Yes
Prices : **Prices for Disabled; Prices for Helpers**: Free of charge for the disabled. Helpers £5.00
Toilets : **Location of Disabled Toilets (+ Number)**: One available 50 yards from the Disabled Area
Blind : **Facilities Available**: No Special Facilities
Bookings : **Are Bookings Necessary**: Yes **Contact Number**: (081) 548-2748

Wigan Athletic FC

Wheelchairs : **Location of Accommodation**: Accommodated - Disabled Unit within Jewsons Enclosure
Nº Spaces for Home Fans; Nº Spaces for Away Fans: 10 spaces in total
Are Helpers Admitted; Nº Admitted: One helper admitted per disabled person
Prices : **Prices for Disabled; Prices for Helpers**: Free of charge for the disabled. Helpers £4.50
Toilets : **Location of Disabled Toilets (+ Number)**: None
Blind : **Facilities Available**: Commentaries Available in Phoenix Stand
Bookings : **Are Bookings Necessary**: Yes **Contact Number**: (0942) 44433

Wimbledon FC

Wheelchairs : **Location of Accommodation**: In Disabled Section - Arthur Wait Stand (Park Road Entrance)
Nº Spaces for Home Fans; Nº Spaces for Away Fans: 28 spaces available in total
Are Helpers Admitted; Nº Admitted: One helper admitted per disabled supporter
Prices : **Prices for Disabled; Prices for Helpers**: Disabled Free of charge. Helpers concessionary price
Toilets : **Location of Disabled Toilets (+ Number)**: Located in Disabled Section
Blind : **Facilities Available**: Commentaries Available - 6 places
Bookings : **Are Bookings Necessary**: Yes **Contact Number**: (081) 771-8841

Wolverhampton Wanderers FC

Wheelchairs : **Location of Accommodation**: Accommodated in Disabled Section - Stan Cullis Stand
Nº Spaces for Home Fans; Nº Spaces for Away Fans: 50 spaces available in total
Are Helpers Admitted; Nº Admitted: One helper admitted per wheelchair
Prices : **Prices for Disabled; Prices for Helpers**: Free of charge for the disabled. £6.00 for helpers
Toilets : **Location of Disabled Toilets (+ Number)**: Toilets at both ends of Stan Cullis Stand
Blind : **Facilities Available**: Commentary by local blind organisation
Bookings : **Are Bookings Necessary**: No **Contact Number**: (0902) 25899

Wrexham FC

Wheelchairs : **Location of Accommodation**: Accommodated in Disabled Section - Mold Road Side
Nº Spaces for Home Fans; Nº Spaces for Away Fans: 18 spaces in total
Are Helpers Admitted; Nº Admitted: One helper admitted per wheelchair
Prices : **Prices for Disabled; Prices for Helpers**: Free of charge for the disabled. £6.00 per helper
Toilets : **Location of Disabled Toilets (+ Number)**: Available in Disabled Section - Mold Road Side
Blind : **Facilities Available**: Commentaries Available (By Hospital Radio Broadcasters)
Bookings : **Are Bookings Necessary**: Yes **Contact Number**: (0978) 351332

Wycombe Wanderers FC

Wheelchairs : **Location of Accommodation**: Pitchside enclosure by Main Stand
Nº Spaces for Home Fans; Nº Spaces for Away Fans: 6 spaces available in total
Are Helpers Admitted; Nº Admitted: One helper admitted per wheelchair
Prices : **Prices for Disabled; Prices for Helpers**: £3.50 for the disabled. Full price for helpers
Toilets : **Location of Disabled Toilets (+ Number)**: Available at rear of Pitchside enclosure
Blind : **Facilities Available**: 4 seats with headsets available
Bookings : **Are Bookings Necessary**: Yes **Contact Number**: (0494) 472100

York City FC

Wheelchairs : **Location of Accommodation**: Accommodated in Disabled Section - In front of Family Stand
Nº Spaces for Home Fans; Nº Spaces for Away Fans: 18 spaces available in total
Are Helpers Admitted; Nº Admitted: One helper admitted per disabled person
Prices : **Prices for Disabled; Prices for Helpers**: Free of charge for the disabled. Helpers £6.50
Toilets : **Location of Disabled Toilets (+ Number)**: Available at entrance to Disabled Area
Blind : **Facilities Available**: Commentaries Available
Bookings : **Are Bookings Necessary**: No **Contact Number**: (0904) 624447

Scottish Football League Clubs

Aberdeen FC

Wheelchairs : **Location of Accommodation**: In front of Richard Donald Stand & Merkland Stand
Nº Spaces for Home Fans; Nº Spaces for Away Fans: 28 spaces available in total
Are Helpers Admitted; Nº Admitted: One helper admitted per wheelchair
Prices : **Prices for Disabled; Prices for Helpers**: Free of charge for the disabled. Full-price helpers
Toilets : **Location of Disabled Toilets (+ Number)**: 1 in Richard Donald Stand. 1 by Merkland Stand
Blind : **Facilities Available**: Special facilities may be available by Arrangement
Bookings : **Are Bookings Necessary**: Yes (1 week) **Contact Number**: (0224) 632328

Airdrieonians FC

Wheelchairs : **Location of Accommodation**: Accommodated in the front sections of both stands
Nº Spaces for Home Fans; Nº Spaces for Away Fans: 10 spaces each for home & away fans
Are Helpers Admitted; Nº Admitted: One helper admitted per disabled supporter
Prices : **Prices for Disabled; Prices for Helpers**: Free of charge for the disabled. £6.00 for helpers
Toilets : **Location of Disabled Toilets (+ Number)**: 4 available in the Main Stand & West Stand
Blind : **Facilities Available**: No Special Facilities
Bookings : **Are Bookings Necessary**: No **Contact Number**: (0236) 451511

Albion Rovers FC

Wheelchairs : **Location of Accommodation**: Accommodated in Disabled Section
Nº Spaces for Home Fans; Nº Spaces for Away Fans: Approximately 30 spaces available.
Are Helpers Admitted; Nº Admitted: One helper admitted per disabled supporter
Prices : **Prices for Disabled; Prices for Helpers**: £5.00 each for the disabled and helpers
Toilets : **Location of Disabled Toilets (+ Number)**: One available at the East End of the Ground
Blind : **Facilities Available**: No Special Facilities
Bookings : **Are Bookings Necessary**: Preferred **Contact Number**: (0236) 432350

Alloa Athletic FC

Wheelchairs : **Location of Accommodation**: Accommodated in Disabled Section underneath the Main Stand
Nº Spaces for Home Fans; Nº Spaces for Away Fans: Not specified
Are Helpers Admitted; Nº Admitted: One helper admitted per disabled supporter
Prices : **Prices for Disabled; Prices for Helpers**: Free of charge for both the disabled and helpers
Toilets : **Location of Disabled Toilets (+ Number)**: One available underneath Main Stand
Blind : **Facilities Available**: No Special Facilities
Bookings : **Are Bookings Necessary**: No **Contact Number**: (0259) 722695

Arbroath FC

Wheelchairs : **Location of Accommodation**: Accommodated at the West End of the Main Stand
Nº Spaces for Home Fans; Nº Spaces for Away Fans: 10 spaces available in total
Are Helpers Admitted; Nº Admitted: One helper admitted with each disabled supporter
Prices : **Prices for Disabled; Prices for Helpers**: Normal prices for both the disabled and helpers
Toilets : **Location of Disabled Toilets (+ Number)**: One available by the Club Shop
Blind : **Facilities Available**: No Special Facilities
Bookings : **Are Bookings Necessary**: No **Contact Number**: (0241) 872157

Ayr United FC

Wheelchairs : **Location of Accommodation**: Accommodated in Disabled Section beneath Family Stand
Nº Spaces for Home Fans; Nº Spaces for Away Fans: 30 spaces available in total
Are Helpers Admitted; Nº Admitted: One helper admitted per disabled supporter
Prices : **Prices for Disabled; Prices for Helpers**: Phone for details
Toilets : **Location of Disabled Toilets (+ Number)**: 2 Gents & 1 Ladies available in Disabled Section
Blind : **Facilities Available**: Commentary may be available - phone club for details
Bookings : **Are Bookings Necessary**: All-ticket games only **Contact Number**: (0292) 263435

Berwick Rangers FC

Wheelchairs : **Location of Accommodation**: Accommodated by the Main Stand
Nº Spaces for Home Fans; Nº Spaces for Away Fans: Not limited
Are Helpers Admitted; Nº Admitted: Yes
Prices : **Prices for Disabled; Prices for Helpers**: £2.50 each for disabled and helpers
Toilets : **Location of Disabled Toilets (+ Number)**: Available in General toilet block
Blind : **Facilities Available**: No Special Facilities
Bookings : **Are Bookings Necessary**: Yes **Contact Number**: (0289) 307424 or 307623

Brechin City FC

Wheelchairs : **Location of Accommodation**: Accommodated in front of the Seated Enclosure
Nº Spaces for Home Fans; Nº Spaces for Away Fans: 10 spaces each for home & away fans
Are Helpers Admitted; Nº Admitted: One helper admitted per disabled spectator
Prices : **Prices for Disabled; Prices for Helpers**: £2.50 each for disabled fans and helpers
Toilets : **Location of Disabled Toilets (+ Number)**: 2 available within the Covered Enclosure
Blind : **Facilities Available**: No Special Facilities
Bookings : **Are Bookings Necessary**: Yes **Contact Number**: (0356) 622942

CALEDONIAN THISTLE FC

WHEELCHAIRS : **Location of Accommodation**: Accommodated around Ground
Nº Spaces for Home Fans; Away Fans: No specific number
Are Helpers Admitted; Nº Admitted: Yes
PRICES : **Prices for Disabled; Prices for Helpers**: Normal prices for both the disabled and helpers
TOILETS : **Location of Disabled Toilets (+ Number)**: None
BLIND : **Facilities Available**: No Special Facilities
BOOKINGS : **Are Bookings Necessary**: Yes **CONTACT NUMBER**: (0463) 233671

CELTIC FC

WHEELCHAIRS : **Location of Accommodation**: Accommodated in both support areas
Nº Spaces for Home Fans; Nº Spaces for Away Fans: 66 spaces for home fans; 5 for away
Are Helpers Admitted; Nº Admitted: 44 helpers admitted for home fans; 5 for away fans
PRICES : **Prices for Disabled; Prices for Helpers**: Free of charge for both the disabled and helpers
TOILETS : **Location of Disabled Toilets (+ Number)**: 5 toilets available in the North Seated Stand
BLIND : **Facilities Available**: Please contact the club for details
BOOKINGS : **Are Bookings Necessary**: Yes **CONTACT NUMBER**: (041) 556-2611 ext. 210

CLYDE FC

WHEELCHAIRS : **Location of Accommodation**: Accommodated in the front sections of both stands
Nº Spaces for Home Fans; Nº Spaces for Away Fans: 10 spaces each for home & away fans
Are Helpers Admitted; Nº Admitted: One helper admitted per disabled supporter
PRICES : **Prices for Disabled; Prices for Helpers**: Free of charge for the disabled. £6.00 for helpers
TOILETS : **Location of Disabled Toilets (+ Number)**: 4 available in the Main Stand & West Stand
BLIND : **Facilities Available**: No Special Facilities
BOOKINGS : **Are Bookings Necessary**: No **CONTACT NUMBER**: (0236) 451511

CLYDEBANK FC

WHEELCHAIRS : **Location of Accommodation**: Accommodated at the back of the Bankies Club Stand
Nº Spaces for Home Fans; Nº Spaces for Away Fans: 12 spaces available in total
Are Helpers Admitted; Nº Admitted: One helper admitted per disabled supporter
PRICES : **Prices for Disabled; Prices for Helpers**: Normally free of charge for the disabled and helpers
TOILETS : **Location of Disabled Toilets (+ Number)**: None available
BLIND : **Facilities Available**: Commentary may be available. Please contact the club for details
BOOKINGS : **Are Bookings Necessary**: Yes **CONTACT NUMBER**: (041) 952-2887

COWDENBEATH FC

WHEELCHAIRS : **Location of Accommodation**: Accommodated in the New Stand
Nº Spaces for Home Fans; Nº Spaces for Away Fans: 3 spaces each for home & away fans
Are Helpers Admitted; Nº Admitted: One helper admitted per disabled supporter
PRICES : **Prices for Disabled; Prices for Helpers**: Free of charge for both the disabled and helpers
TOILETS : **Location of Disabled Toilets (+ Number)**: 1 Ladies, 1 Gents & 1 Communal in New Stand
BLIND : **Facilities Available**: No Special facilities
BOOKINGS : **Are Bookings Necessary**: Yes **CONTACT NUMBER**: (0383) 610166

DUMBARTON FC

WHEELCHAIRS : **Location of Accommodation**: Disabled supporters are accommodated trackside
Nº Spaces for Home Fans; Nº Spaces for Away Fans: 3 spaces available for home fans only
Are Helpers Admitted; Nº Admitted: One helper admitted per wheelchair
PRICES : **Prices for Disabled; Prices for Helpers**: £2.50 per disabled person. £5.00 per helper
TOILETS : **Location of Disabled Toilets (+ Number)**: One available in the Main Stand
BLIND : **Facilities Available**: No Special Facilities
BOOKINGS : **Are Bookings Necessary**: No **CONTACT NUMBER**: (0389) 62569

DUNDEE FC

WHEELCHAIRS : **Location of Accommodation**: Accommodated in the Family Stand
Nº Spaces for Home Fans; Nº Spaces for Away Fans: Not specified
Are Helpers Admitted; Nº Admitted: Yes
PRICES : **Prices for Disabled; Prices for Helpers**: Phone for details
TOILETS : **Location of Disabled Toilets (+ Number)**: Should become available during 1994/95 season
BLIND : **Facilities Available**: No Special Facilities
BOOKINGS : **Are Bookings Necessary**: Yes **CONTACT NUMBER**: (0382) 826104

DUNDEE UNITED FC

WHEELCHAIRS : **Location of Accommodation**: Accommodated in the George Fox Stand
Nº Spaces for Home Fans; Nº Spaces for Away Fans: Not specified
Are Helpers Admitted; Nº Admitted: One helper admitted per wheelchair
PRICES : **Prices for Disabled; Prices for Helpers**: Disabled - free of charge. Helpers - £8.00
TOILETS : **Location of Disabled Toilets (+ Number)**: 2 available within the George Fox Stand
BLIND : **Facilities Available**: Commentary may be available. Contact the club for details
BOOKINGS : **Are Bookings Necessary**: Yes **CONTACT NUMBER**: (0382) 833166

DUNFERMLINE FC

WHEELCHAIRS : **Location of Accommodation**: Not specified
Nº Spaces for Home Fans; Nº Spaces for Away Fans: 15 spaces each for home & away fans
Are Helpers Admitted; Nº Admitted: One helper admitted per disabled supporter
PRICES : **Prices for Disabled; Prices for Helpers**: Free of Charge for both disabled & helpers
TOILETS : **Location of Disabled Toilets (+ Number)**: One available in the West End Stand
BLIND : **Facilities Available**: Free admission to West End Stand
BOOKINGS : **Are Bookings Necessary**: No **CONTACT NUMBER**: (0383) 772778

EAST FIFE FC

WHEELCHAIRS : **Location of Accommodation**: Accommodated at the end of the Grandstand
Nº Spaces for Home Fans; Nº Spaces for Away Fans: 20 spaces for home fans; 10 for away
Are Helpers Admitted; Nº Admitted: Yes
PRICES : **Prices for Disabled; Prices for Helpers**: Free of charge for the disabled. Helpers half-price
TOILETS : **Location of Disabled Toilets (+ Number)**: 2 available behind the Grandstand
BLIND : **Facilities Available**: No Special Facilities
BOOKINGS : **Are Bookings Necessary**: 1 week in advance **CONTACT NUMBER**: (0333) 426323

EAST STIRLINGSHIRE FC

WHEELCHAIRS : **Location of Accommodation**: Not specified
Nº Spaces for Home Fans; Nº Spaces for Away Fans: Not specified
Are Helpers Admitted; Nº Admitted: As many helpers as necessary are admitted
PRICES : **Prices for Disabled; Prices for Helpers**: £4.00 each for both the disabled and helpers
TOILETS : **Location of Disabled Toilets (+ Number)**: Available in the Main Stand
BLIND : **Facilities Available**: No Special Facilities
BOOKINGS : **Are Bookings Necessary**: Yes **CONTACT NUMBER**: (0324) 623583

FALKIRK FC

WHEELCHAIRS : **Location of Accommodation**: Accommodated by prior arrangement
Nº Spaces for Home Fans; Nº Spaces for Away Fans: No specific numbers
Are Helpers Admitted; Nº Admitted: Yes
PRICES : **Prices for Disabled; Prices for Helpers**: Phone for details
TOILETS : **Location of Disabled Toilets (+ Number)**: None
BLIND : **Facilities Available**: No Special Facilities
BOOKINGS : **Are Bookings Necessary**: Yes **CONTACT NUMBER**: (0324) 24121

FORFAR ATHLETIC FC

WHEELCHAIRS : **Location of Accommodation**: Accommodated to the West of the Main Stand
Nº Spaces for Home Fans; Nº Spaces for Away Fans: 4 spaces each for home & away fans
Are Helpers Admitted; Nº Admitted: One helper admitted per disabled supporter
PRICES : **Prices for Disabled; Prices for Helpers**: Free of charge for the disabled. £4.00 for helpers
TOILETS : **Location of Disabled Toilets (+ Number)**: One available
BLIND : **Facilities Available**: No Special Facilities
BOOKINGS : **Are Bookings Necessary**: No **CONTACT NUMBER**: (0307) 464924

GREENOCK MORTON FC

WHEELCHAIRS : **Location of Accommodation**: Accommodated below the Grandstand
Nº Spaces for Home Fans; Nº Spaces for Away Fans: 5 spaces each for home & away fans
Are Helpers Admitted; Nº Admitted: One helper admitted per disabled supporter
PRICES : **Prices for Disabled; Prices for Helpers**: Free of charge for the disabled. Helpers full-price
TOILETS : **Location of Disabled Toilets (+ Number)**: None
BLIND : **Facilities Available**: Commentaries may be available. Contact the club for further details
BOOKINGS : **Are Bookings Necessary**: No **CONTACT NUMBER**: (0475) 723571

Hamilton Academical FC

Wheelchairs : **Location of Accommodation**: Accommodated at the front of the New Stand
Nº Spaces for Home Fans; Nº Spaces for Away Fans: 8 spaces available in total
Are Helpers Admitted; Nº Admitted: One helper admitted for each wheelchair
Prices : **Prices for Disabled; Prices for Helpers**: Free of charge for both the disabled and helpers
Toilets : **Location of Disabled Toilets (+ Number)**: One available ten yards from disabled enclosure
Blind : **Facilities Available**: No Special Facilities but will accommodate if asked
Bookings : **Are Bookings Necessary**: Yes **Contact Number**: (0698) 286103

Heart of Midlothian FC

Wheelchairs : **Location of Accommodation**: Home fans in South Enclosure. Away fans in the Family Area
Nº Spaces for Home Fans; Nº Spaces for Away Fans: 12 spaces for home fans; 8 for away
Are Helpers Admitted; Nº Admitted: One helper admitted for each wheelchair
Prices : **Prices for Disabled; Prices for Helpers**: Free of charge for the disabled. Full price for helpers
Toilets : **Location of Disabled Toilets (+ Number)**: 2 available in the South Enclosure
Blind : **Facilities Available**: Commentary may be available. Contact the club for details
Bookings : **Are Bookings Necessary**: Yes **Contact Number**: (031) 337-6132

Hibernian FC

Wheelchairs : **Location of Accommodation**: Accommodated in the South Seated Enclosure
Nº Spaces for Home Fans; Nº Spaces for Away Fans: 16 spaces available in total
Are Helpers Admitted; Nº Admitted: 16 helpers admitted in total
Prices : **Prices for Disabled; Prices for Helpers**: Free of charge for the disabled. £7.00 for helpers
Toilets : **Location of Disabled Toilets (+ Number)**: One available in the South Seated Enclosure
Blind : **Facilities Available**: 10 seats available in the North Stand
Bookings : **Are Bookings Necessary**: No **Contact Number**: (031) 661-2159

Kilmarnock FC

Wheelchairs : **Location of Accommodation**: Accommodated in the Main Stand
Nº Spaces for Home Fans; Nº Spaces for Away Fans: 8 spaces for home fans; 4 for away
Are Helpers Admitted; Nº Admitted: One helper admitted for each Wheelchair
Prices : **Prices for Disabled; Prices for Helpers**: Free of charge for both the disabled and helpers
Toilets : **Location of Disabled Toilets (+ Number)**: One available in the Main Stand
Blind : **Facilities Available**: No Special Facilities
Bookings : **Are Bookings Necessary**: Yes **Contact Number**: (0563) 25184

Meadowbank Thistle FC

Wheelchairs : **Location of Accommodation**: Accommodated in the Main Stand
Nº Spaces for Home Fans; Nº Spaces for Away Fans: Not specified
Are Helpers Admitted; Nº Admitted: Yes
Prices : **Prices for Disabled; Prices for Helpers**: Free of charge for disabled. Normal price for helpers
Toilets : **Location of Disabled Toilets (+ Number)**: Disabled toilets available
Blind : **Facilities Available**: No Special Facilities
Bookings : **Are Bookings Necessary**: Yes **Contact Number**: (031) 661-5351

Montrose FC

Wheelchairs : **Location of Accommodation**: Not specified
Nº Spaces for Home Fans; Nº Spaces for Away Fans: 5 spaces available for home fans only
Are Helpers Admitted; Nº Admitted: One helper admitted per disabled supporter
Prices : **Prices for Disabled; Prices for Helpers**: £2.50 or £4.00 for the disabled and helpers
Toilets : **Location of Disabled Toilets (+ Number)**: 2 available
Blind : **Facilities Available**: No Special Facilities
Bookings : **Are Bookings Necessary**: Helpful **Contact Number**: (0674) 673200

Motherwell FC

Wheelchairs : **Location of Accommodation**: Accommodated in South-West Enclosure
Nº Spaces for Home Fans; Nº Spaces for Away Fans: 12 spaces home fans; 6 for away
Are Helpers Admitted; Nº Admitted: One helper admitted per disabled person
Prices : **Prices for Disabled; Prices for Helpers**: Free of charge for both the disabled and helpers
Toilets : **Location of Disabled Toilets (+ Number)**: One available close to the disabled area
Blind : **Facilities Available**: No Special Facilities
Bookings : **Are Bookings Necessary**: 1 week's notice **Contact Number**: (0698) 261437

Partick Thistle FC

Wheelchairs : **Location of Accommodation**: Accommodated in North Enclosure
Nº Spaces for Home Fans; Nº Spaces for Away Fans: 10 spaces available in total
Are Helpers Admitted; Nº Admitted: One helper admitted per disabled supporter
Prices : **Prices for Disabled; Prices for Helpers**: Free of charge for the disabled. £7 or £8 for helpers
Toilets : **Location of Disabled Toilets (+ Number)**: One available in Main Stand area
Blind : **Facilities Available**: Facilities may be available on request
Bookings : **Are Bookings Necessary**: Yes **Contact Number**: (041) 945-4811

Queen of the South FC

Wheelchairs : **Location of Accommodation**: Accommodated in front of the Terracing
Nº Spaces for Home Fans; Nº Spaces for Away Fans: Not specified
Are Helpers Admitted; Nº Admitted: One helper admitted per disabled person
Prices : **Prices for Disabled; Prices for Helpers**: Free of charge for the disabled. £4.00 for helpers
Toilets : **Location of Disabled Toilets (+ Number)**: None (wheelchairs have access to a normal toilet)
Blind : **Facilities Available**: No Special Facilities
Bookings : **Are Bookings Necessary**: No **Contact Number**: (0387) 54853

Queen's Park FC

Wheelchairs : **Location of Accommodation**: Accommodated on the Disabled Terrace - South Stand
Nº Spaces for Home Fans; Nº Spaces for Away Fans: 54 spaces available in total
Are Helpers Admitted; Nº Admitted: No
Prices : **Prices for Disabled; Prices for Helpers**: Free of charge for the disabled
Toilets : **Location of Disabled Toilets (+ Number)**: Two available in the Disabled Terrace
Blind : **Facilities Available**: Commentaries may be available. Contact the club for details
Bookings : **Are Bookings Necessary**: Yes **Contact Number**: (041) 632-1275

Raith Rovers FC

Wheelchairs : **Location of Accommodation**: Accommodated on the North-East Trackside
Nº Spaces for Home Fans; Nº Spaces for Away Fans: 10 spaces each for home & away fans
Are Helpers Admitted; Nº Admitted: No limit on the number of helpers (within reason)
Prices : **Prices for Disabled; Prices for Helpers**: Free of charge for the disabled. £7.00 for helpers
Toilets : **Location of Disabled Toilets (+ Number)**: None
Blind : **Facilities Available**: No Special Facilities
Bookings : **Are Bookings Necessary**: Yes **Contact Number**: (0592) 263514

Rangers FC

Wheelchairs : **Location of Accommodation**: Accommodated in front of the West Enclosure
Nº Spaces for Home Fans; Nº Spaces for Away Fans: Not specified
Are Helpers Admitted; Nº Admitted: Yes - phone for details
Prices : **Prices for Disabled; Prices for Helpers**: Phone for details
Toilets : **Location of Disabled Toilets (+ Number)**: Available in the West Enclosure
Blind : **Facilities Available**: Commentaries available at the East End of the West Enclosure
Bookings : **Are Bookings Necessary**: Yes **Contact Number**: (041) 427-8500

Ross County FC

Wheelchairs : **Location of Accommodation**: Accommodated in the Stand
Nº Spaces for Home Fans; Nº Spaces for Away Fans: 2 spaces each for home & away fans
Are Helpers Admitted; Nº Admitted: One helper admitted per wheelchair
Prices : **Prices for Disabled; Prices for Helpers**: Half-price for both the disabled & helpers
Toilets : **Location of Disabled Toilets (+ Number)**: One available at the bottom of the Stand
Blind : **Facilities Available**: No Special Facilities
Bookings : **Are Bookings Necessary**: Yes **Contact Number**: (0349) 62253

St. Johnstone FC

Wheelchairs : **Location of Accommodation**: Accommodated in the East and West Stands
Nº Spaces for Home Fans; Nº Spaces for Away Fans: 15 spaces each for home & away fans
Are Helpers Admitted; Nº Admitted: One helper admitted per disabled person
Prices : **Prices for Disabled; Prices for Helpers**: £6.00 for the disabled. £7.00 or £10.00 for helpers
Toilets : **Location of Disabled Toilets (+ Number)**: 2 available in both the East and West Stands
Blind : **Facilities Available**: 24 headphones available around the stadium to listen to live broadcast
Bookings : **Are Bookings Necessary**: Yes **Contact Number**: (0738) 26961

St. Mirren FC

Wheelchairs : **Location of Accommodation**: Accommodated in the New West Stand
Nº Spaces for Home Fans; Nº Spaces for Away Fans: Not specified
Are Helpers Admitted; Nº Admitted: Yes
Prices : **Prices for Disabled; Prices for Helpers**: Normal prices for both the disabled and helpers
Toilets : **Location of Disabled Toilets (+ Number)**: Available in the New West Stand
Blind : **Facilities Available**: No Special Facilities
Bookings : **Are Bookings Necessary**: Yes **Contact Number**: (041) 840-1337

Stenhousemuir FC

Wheelchairs : **Location of Accommodation**: Not specified
Nº Spaces for Home Fans; Nº Spaces for Away Fans: Not specified
Are Helpers Admitted; Nº Admitted: One helper admitted per disabled person
Prices : **Prices for Disabled; Prices for Helpers**: Full-price for both the disabled and helpers
Toilets : **Location of Disabled Toilets (+ Number)**: Available on West Terracing
Blind : **Facilities Available**: No Special Facilities
Bookings : **Are Bookings Necessary**: No **Contact Number**: (0324) 562992

Stirling Albion FC

Wheelchairs : **Location of Accommodation**: Accommodated in front of the Stands
Nº Spaces for Home Fans; Nº Spaces for Away Fans: 18 spaces each for home & away fans
Are Helpers Admitted; Nº Admitted: One helper admitted per disabled supporter
Prices : **Prices for Disabled; Prices for Helpers**: Free of charge for both the disabled & helpers
Toilets : **Location of Disabled Toilets (+ Number)**: 4 available: - 2 beneath each Stand
Blind : **Facilities Available**: No Special Facilities
Bookings : **Are Bookings Necessary**: No **Contact Number**: (0786) 450399

Stranraer FC

Wheelchairs : **Location of Accommodation**: Accommodated in front of the North Stand
Nº Spaces for Home Fans; Nº Spaces for Away Fans: 6 spaces each for home & away fans
Are Helpers Admitted; Nº Admitted: One helper admitted per wheelchair
Prices : **Prices for Disabled; Prices for Helpers**: Phone for details
Toilets : **Location of Disabled Toilets (+ Number)**: One available in the official Disabled Area
Blind : **Facilities Available**: No Special Facilities
Bookings : **Are Bookings Necessary**: Yes **Contact Number**: (0776) 702194

G.M. Vauxhall Conference Clubs

Altrincham FC

Wheelchairs : **Location of Accommodation**: Accommodated adjacent to Away Dug-out
Nº Spaces for Home Fans; Nº Spaces for Away Fans: 3 spaces each for home & away fans
Are Helpers Admitted; Nº Admitted: One helper admitted per disabled supporter
Prices : **Prices for Disabled; Prices for Helpers**: £2.50 each for the disabled fans and for helpers
Toilets : **Location of Disabled Toilets (+ Number)**: None at present
Blind : **Facilities Available**: No Special Facilities
Bookings : **Are Bookings Necessary**: Yes **Contact Number**: (061) 928-1045

Bath City FC

Wheelchairs : **Location of Accommodation**: Accommodated in front of Family Stand
Nº Spaces for Home Fans; Nº Spaces for Away Fans: 10 spaces each for home & away fans
Are Helpers Admitted; Nº Admitted: Helpers admitted by arrangement
Prices : **Prices for Disabled; Prices for Helpers**: Prices determined by arrangement
Toilets : **Location of Disabled Toilets (+ Number)**: 2 available behind the Family Stand
Blind : **Facilities Available**: No special facilities but accommodated by arrangement
Bookings : **Are Bookings Necessary**: Yes **Contact Number**: (0225) 423087

Bromsgrove Rovers FC

Wheelchairs : **Location of Accommodation**: Accommodated outside the Police Control Room
Nº Spaces for Home Fans; Nº Spaces for Away Fans: 6 spaces available (more if necessary)
Are Helpers Admitted; Nº Admitted: One helper admitted per disabled supporter
Prices : **Prices for Disabled; Prices for Helpers**: £4.50 or £2.50 (concessions) for disabled or helpers
Toilets : **Location of Disabled Toilets (+ Number)**: No special toilets. Normal toilets are nearby
Blind : **Facilities Available**: No Special Facilities
Bookings : **Are Bookings Necessary**: Appreciated **Contact Number**: (0527) 876949

Dagenham & Redbridge FC

Wheelchairs : **Location of Accommodation**: Accommodated in South/West End of the Ground
Nº Spaces for Home Fans; Nº Spaces for Away Fans: 10 spaces available in total
Are Helpers Admitted; Nº Admitted: One helper admitted per disabled supporter
Prices : **Prices for Disabled; Prices for Helpers**: Free of charge for disabled. Normal price for helpers
Toilets : **Location of Disabled Toilets (+ Number)**: Available at East and West Ends of the Ground
Blind : **Facilities Available**: No special facilities but stewards will assist if necessary
Bookings : **Are Bookings Necessary**: No **Contact Number**: (081) 592-7194

Dover Athletic FC

Wheelchairs : **Location of Accommodation**: Accommodated at the front of the Stand
Nº Spaces for Home Fans; Nº Spaces for Away Fans: Approx. 20 spaces available in total
Are Helpers Admitted; Nº Admitted: Not specified
Prices : **Prices for Disabled; Prices for Helpers**: Normal prices for the disabled and helpers
Toilets : **Location of Disabled Toilets (+ Number)**: None
Blind : **Facilities Available**: No Special Facilities
Bookings : **Are Bookings Necessary**: No **Contact Number**: (0227) 769708

Farnborough Town FC

Wheelchairs : **Location of Accommodation**: Accommodated in front of the Main Stand
Nº Spaces for Home Fans; Nº Spaces for Away Fans: Not specified
Are Helpers Admitted; Nº Admitted: Yes
Prices : **Prices for Disabled; Prices for Helpers**: Normal prices for both the disabled and helpers
Toilets : **Location of Disabled Toilets (+ Number)**: Yes
Blind : **Facilities Available**: No Special Facilities
Bookings : **Are Bookings Necessary**: Yes **Contact Number**: (0252) 541469

Gateshead FC

Wheelchairs : **Location of Accommodation**: Photo Finish - Trackside
Nº Spaces for Home Fans; Nº Spaces for Away Fans: 5 spaces each for home & away fans
Are Helpers Admitted; Nº Admitted: One helper admitted per disabled person
Prices : **Prices for Disabled; Prices for Helpers**: Normal prices for both the disabled and helpers
Toilets : **Location of Disabled Toilets (+ Number)**: One available in Reception Area
Blind : **Facilities Available**: No Special Facilities
Bookings : **Are Bookings Necessary**: Yes **Contact Number**: (091) 478-3883

Halifax Town FC

Wheelchairs : **Location of Accommodation**: Accommodated in Disabled Section - Family Stand
Nº Spaces for Home Fans; Nº Spaces for Away Fans: 10 spaces available in total
Are Helpers Admitted; Nº Admitted: Yes
Prices : **Prices for Disabled; Prices for Helpers**: 1 disabled & 1 helper costs £7. Extra helpers £6 each
Toilets : **Location of Disabled Toilets (+ Number)**: At end of ramp from Stand
Blind : **Facilities Available**: No Special Facilities
Bookings : **Are Bookings Necessary**: No **Contact Number**: (0422) 353423

Kettering Town FC

Wheelchairs : **Location of Accommodation**: Accommodated on terracing adjacent to the Main Stand
Nº Spaces for Home Fans; Nº Spaces for Away Fans: 12 spaces available in total
Are Helpers Admitted; Nº Admitted: One helper admitted per disabled supporter
Prices : **Prices for Disabled; Prices for Helpers**: Concessionary prices charged for disabled & helpers
Toilets : **Location of Disabled Toilets (+ Number)**: To be built next to the Social Club during 1994
Blind : **Facilities Available**: No special facilities at present
Bookings : **Are Bookings Necessary**: Helpful **Contact Number**: (0536) 83028

KIDDERMINSTER HARRIERS FC

WHEELCHAIRS : **Location of Accommodation**: Accommodated at the front of the Main Stand
Nº Spaces for Home Fans; Nº Spaces for Away Fans: Not specified
Are Helpers Admitted; Nº Admitted: Yes
PRICES : **Prices for Disabled; Prices for Helpers**: Concessions for the disabled. Usual prices for helpers
TOILETS : **Location of Disabled Toilets (+ Number)**: Available by the disabled area
BLIND : **Facilities Available**: No Special Facilities
BOOKINGS : **Are Bookings Necessary**: Yes **CONTACT NUMBER**: (0562) 823931

MACCLESFIELD TOWN FC

WHEELCHAIRS : **Location of Accommodation**: Accommodated in front of Main Stand
Nº Spaces for Home Fans; Nº Spaces for Away Fans: 6 spaces each for home & away fans
Are Helpers Admitted; Nº Admitted: Not specified
PRICES : **Prices for Disabled; Prices for Helpers**: £4.00 each for the disabled and for helpers
TOILETS : **Location of Disabled Toilets (+ Number)**: None
BLIND : **Facilities Available**: No Special Facilities
BOOKINGS : **Are Bookings Necessary**: No **CONTACT NUMBER**: (0623) 511113

MERTHYR TYDFIL FC

WHEELCHAIRS : **Location of Accommodation**: Accommodated at the Front of the Main Grandstand
Nº Spaces for Home Fans; Nº Spaces for Away Fans: 20 spaces available in total
Are Helpers Admitted; Nº Admitted: No practical restriction on number of helpers
PRICES : **Prices for Disabled; Prices for Helpers**: £5.00 each for the disabled and for helpers
TOILETS : **Location of Disabled Toilets (+ Number)**: At Strikers Club
BLIND : **Facilities Available**: Hospital Radio Commentaries available. Contact the club for details
BOOKINGS : **Are Bookings Necessary**: No **CONTACT NUMBER**: (0685) 384102

NORTHWICH VICTORIA FC

WHEELCHAIRS : **Location of Accommodation**: Accommodated in front of the Main Stand
Nº Spaces for Home Fans; Nº Spaces for Away Fans: Not Specified
Are Helpers Admitted; Nº Admitted: Helpers admitted - unspecified number
PRICES : **Prices for Disabled; Prices for Helpers**: Full price for both the disabled and helpers
TOILETS : **Location of Disabled Toilets (+ Number)**: None
BLIND : **Facilities Available**: No Special Facilities
BOOKINGS : **Are Bookings Necessary**: No **CONTACT NUMBER**: (0606) 41450

RUNCORN FC

WHEELCHAIRS : **Location of Accommodation**: RUNCORN FC'S MAIN STAND BURNT DOWN
Nº Spaces for Home Fans; Nº Spaces for Away Fans: DURING THE 1993/94 SEASON
Are Helpers Admitted; Nº Admitted: AND THEY ARE GROUND-SHARING WITH
PRICES : **Prices for Disabled; Prices for Helpers**: WITTON ALBION UNTIL 1995.
TOILETS : **Location of Disabled Toilets (+ Number)**: SEE THE WITTON ALBION ENTRY
BLIND : **Facilities Available**: FOR DETAILS.
BOOKINGS : **Are Bookings Necessary**: **CONTACT NUMBER**: (0928) 560076

SOUTHPORT FC

WHEELCHAIRS : **Location of Accommodation**: Accommodated in Blowick End of the Stand
Nº Spaces for Home Fans; Nº Spaces for Away Fans: Not specified
Are Helpers Admitted; Nº Admitted: Helpers admitted as needed
PRICES : **Prices for Disabled; Prices for Helpers**: £4.00 each for the disabled and for helpers
TOILETS : **Location of Disabled Toilets (+ Number)**: One available at the Blowick End of the Stand
BLIND : **Facilities Available**: No Special Facilities
BOOKINGS : **Are Bookings Necessary**: No **CONTACT NUMBER**: (0704) 533422

STAFFORD RANGERS FC

WHEELCHAIRS : **Location of Accommodation**: Accommodated at Marston Road End by the players tunnel
Nº Spaces for Home Fans; Nº Spaces for Away Fans: 15 spaces available in total
Are Helpers Admitted; Nº Admitted: One helper admitted for each wheelchair
PRICES : **Prices for Disabled; Prices for Helpers**: Child/OAP price for disabled. Full price for helpers
TOILETS : **Location of Disabled Toilets (+ Number)**: None
BLIND : **Facilities Available**: Facilities may be available by arrangement
BOOKINGS : **Are Bookings Necessary**: Yes **CONTACT NUMBER**: (0785) 42750

Stalybridge Celtic FC

Wheelchairs : **Location of Accommodation**: Accommodated in the Town End of the Main Stand
Nº Spaces for Home Fans; Nº Spaces for Away Fans: 20 spaces each for home & away fans
Are Helpers Admitted; Nº Admitted: No limit on the number of helpers admitted
Prices : **Prices for Disabled; Prices for Helpers**: Normal prices for the disabled and helpers
Toilets : **Location of Disabled Toilets (+ Number)**: 1 at rear of Main Stand. More being built in '94/95
Blind : **Facilities Available**: Facilities may be available by arrangement - notice required
Bookings : **Are Bookings Necessary**: Helpful **Contact Number**: (061) 338-2828

Stevenage Borough FC

Wheelchairs : **Location of Accommodation**: Accommodated in front of the Stand
Nº Spaces for Home Fans; Nº Spaces for Away Fans: No specific number
Are Helpers Admitted; Nº Admitted: Yes
Prices : **Prices for Disabled; Prices for Helpers**: Normal prices for both the disabled and helpers
Toilets : **Location of Disabled Toilets (+ Number)**: Disabled toilets available
Blind : **Facilities Available**: No Special Facilities
Bookings : **Are Bookings Necessary**: Yes **Contact Number**: (0438) 743322

Telford United FC

Wheelchairs : **Location of Accommodation**: Accommodated at the South End of the Ground
Nº Spaces for Home Fans; Nº Spaces for Away Fans: Not specified
Are Helpers Admitted; Nº Admitted: Maximum of three helpers admitted
Prices : **Prices for Disabled; Prices for Helpers**: Free of charge for the disabled. Helpers £4 or £2
Toilets : **Location of Disabled Toilets (+ Number)**: None
Blind : **Facilities Available**: No Special Facilities
Bookings : **Are Bookings Necessary**: Yes **Contact Number**: (0952) 223838

Welling United FC

Wheelchairs : **Location of Accommodation**: Accommodated at the side of the Main Stand
Nº Spaces for Home Fans; Nº Spaces for Away Fans: Not specified
Are Helpers Admitted; Nº Admitted: Yes
Prices : **Prices for Disabled; Prices for Helpers**: Free of charge for disabled. Usual prices for helpers
Toilets : **Location of Disabled Toilets (+ Number)**: Disabled toilets available
Blind : **Facilities Available**: No Special Facilities
Bookings : **Are Bookings Necessary**: Yes **Contact Number**: (081) 301-1196

Woking FC

Wheelchairs : **Location of Accommodation**: Accommodated on the Touchline (no cover)
Nº Spaces for Home Fans; Nº Spaces for Away Fans: 2 spaces each for home & away fans
Are Helpers Admitted; Nº Admitted: One helper admitted per disabled supporter
Prices : **Prices for Disabled; Prices for Helpers**: £4.50 adult or £2.80 child/OAP for disabled & helpers
Toilets : **Location of Disabled Toilets (+ Number)**: One available by the Club Shop
Blind : **Facilities Available**: No Special Facilities
Bookings : **Are Bookings Necessary**: Yes **Contact Number**: (0483) 772470

Yeovil Town FC

Wheelchairs : **Location of Accommodation**: Not specified
Nº Spaces for Home Fans; Nº Spaces for Away Fans: 8 spaces each for home & away fans
Are Helpers Admitted; Nº Admitted: No limit to number of helpers admitted (within reason)
Prices : **Prices for Disabled; Prices for Helpers**: Normal prices for the disabled and helpers
Toilets : **Location of Disabled Toilets (+ Number)**: 2 available
Blind : **Facilities Available**: No Special Facilities
Bookings : **Are Bookings Necessary**: No **Contact Number**: (0935) 23662

Diadora League Premier Division Clubs

Aylesbury United FC

Wheelchairs :	**Location of Accommodation**: Not specified. Will accommodate and charge depending
	Nº Spaces for Home Fans; Nº Spaces for Away Fans: on the circumstances
	Are Helpers Admitted; Nº Admitted: Everyone will be catered for
Prices :	**Prices for Disabled; Prices for Helpers**: See above
Toilets :	**Location of Disabled Toilets (+ Number)**: 1 in each of Gents and Ladies toilets in clubhouse
Blind :	**Facilities Available**: No Special Facilities
Bookings :	**Are Bookings Necessary**: Yes **Contact Number**: (0296) 436350

Bishop's Stortford FC

Wheelchairs :	**Location of Accommodation**: Accommodated in front of the Clubhouse Stand
	Nº Spaces for Home Fans; Nº Spaces for Away Fans: Not specified
	Are Helpers Admitted; Nº Admitted: Yes
Prices :	**Prices for Disabled; Prices for Helpers**: Normal prices for both the disabled and helpers
Toilets :	**Location of Disabled Toilets (+ Number)**: None
Blind :	**Facilities Available**: No Special Facilities
Bookings :	**Are Bookings Necessary**: Yes **Contact Number**: (0279) 654140

Bromley FC

Wheelchairs :	**Location of Accommodation**: Not specified
	Nº Spaces for Home Fans; Nº Spaces for Away Fans: Not specified
	Are Helpers Admitted; Nº Admitted: Practically no limits on the number of helpers
Prices :	**Prices for Disabled; Prices for Helpers**: Normal prices for both the disabled and helpers
Toilets :	**Location of Disabled Toilets (+ Number)**: None
Blind :	**Facilities Available**: No Special Facilities
Bookings :	**Are Bookings Necessary**: No **Contact Number**: (081) 460-5291

Carshalton Athletic FC

Wheelchairs :	**Location of Accommodation**: Accommodated at the End of the Stand
	Nº Spaces for Home Fans; Nº Spaces for Away Fans: 6 spaces each for home & away fans
	Are Helpers Admitted; Nº Admitted: Maximum of 12 helpers admitted
Prices :	**Prices for Disabled; Prices for Helpers**: £1.50 each for both the disabled and the helpers
Toilets :	**Location of Disabled Toilets (+ Number)**: None
Blind :	**Facilities Available**: No Special Facilities
Bookings :	**Are Bookings Necessary**: No **Contact Number**: (081) 770-3692

Chesham United FC

Wheelchairs :	**Location of Accommodation**: Accommodated in corner of Ground at Meadow End
	Nº Spaces for Home Fans; Nº Spaces for Away Fans: 5 spaces each for home & away fans
	Are Helpers Admitted; Nº Admitted: Maximum of 10 helpers admitted
Prices :	**Prices for Disabled; Prices for Helpers**: Free of charge for both the disabled and helpers
Toilets :	**Location of Disabled Toilets (+ Number)**: None
Blind :	**Facilities Available**: No Special Facilities
Bookings :	**Are Bookings Necessary**: Yes **Contact Number**: (0494) 783964

Dulwich Hamlet FC

Wheelchairs :	**Location of Accommodation**: Accommodated in front of the Bar in the Stand Enclosure
	Nº Spaces for Home Fans; Nº Spaces for Away Fans: 10 spaces available in total
	Are Helpers Admitted; Nº Admitted: Not specified
Prices :	**Prices for Disabled; Prices for Helpers**: Free of charge for both the disabled and helpers
Toilets :	**Location of Disabled Toilets (+ Number)**: Easy access in club behind Disabled Enclosure
Blind :	**Facilities Available**: No Special Facilities
Bookings :	**Are Bookings Necessary**: Yes **Contact Number**: (071) 274-8707

ENFIELD FC

WHEELCHAIRS : **Location of Accommodation**: Accommodated adjacent to Starlight Suite (no cover)
Nº Spaces for Home Fans; Nº Spaces for Away Fans: 5 spaces each for home & away fans
Are Helpers Admitted; Nº Admitted: Two helpers admitted per wheelchair
PRICES : **Prices for Disabled; Prices for Helpers**: Free of charge for disabled. Normal price for helpers
TOILETS : **Location of Disabled Toilets (+ Number)**: None
BLIND : **Facilities Available**: Facilities may be available by arrangement
BOOKINGS : **Are Bookings Necessary**: Helpful **CONTACT NUMBER**: (081) 292-0665

GRAYS ATHLETIC FC

WHEELCHAIRS : **Location of Accommodation**: Accommodated in Stand by the Club Shop
Nº Spaces for Home Fans; Nº Spaces for Away Fans: Not specified
Are Helpers Admitted; Nº Admitted: As many helpers as necessary are admitted
PRICES : **Prices for Disabled; Prices for Helpers**: Free for the disabled. Normal prices for helpers
TOILETS : **Location of Disabled Toilets (+ Number)**: None
BLIND : **Facilities Available**: No Special Facilities
BOOKINGS : **Are Bookings Necessary**: No **CONTACT NUMBER**: (0375) 391649

HARROW BOROUGH FC

WHEELCHAIRS : **Location of Accommodation**: No special facilities for the disabled
Nº Spaces for Home Fans; Nº Spaces for Away Fans: -
Are Helpers Admitted; Nº Admitted: -
PRICES : **Prices for Disabled; Prices for Helpers**: Normal prices for the disabled
TOILETS : **Location of Disabled Toilets (+ Number)**: None
BLIND : **Facilities Available**: No Special Facilities
BOOKINGS : **Are Bookings Necessary**: No **CONTACT NUMBER**: -

HAYES FC

WHEELCHAIRS : **Location of Accommodation**: No specific area, but can be accommodated where necessary
Nº Spaces for Home Fans; Nº Spaces for Away Fans: Not specified
Are Helpers Admitted; Nº Admitted: Yes
PRICES : **Prices for Disabled; Prices for Helpers**: £3.50 each for the disabled and the helpers
TOILETS : **Location of Disabled Toilets (+ Number)**: None
BLIND : **Facilities Available**: Facilities available by arrangement
BOOKINGS : **Are Bookings Necessary**: Yes **CONTACT NUMBER**: (081) 573-4598

HENDON FC

WHEELCHAIRS : **Location of Accommodation**: Accommodated at the side of the Main Stand
Nº Spaces for Home Fans; Nº Spaces for Away Fans: 30 spaces available in total
Are Helpers Admitted; Nº Admitted: One helper admitted free per disabled supporter
PRICES : **Prices for Disabled; Prices for Helpers**: Free of charge for the disabled and helpers
TOILETS : **Location of Disabled Toilets (+ Number)**: None
BLIND : **Facilities Available**: No special facilities, but full help and cooperation given on request
BOOKINGS : **Are Bookings Necessary**: Preferred **CONTACT NUMBER**: (081) 201-9494

HITCHIN TOWN FC

WHEELCHAIRS : **Location of Accommodation**: Accommodated at the ends of the Main Stand
Nº Spaces for Home Fans; Nº Spaces for Away Fans: Not specified
Are Helpers Admitted; Nº Admitted: Yes
PRICES : **Prices for Disabled; Prices for Helpers**: Concession prices for disabled. Usual prices helpers
TOILETS : **Location of Disabled Toilets (+ Number)**: Disabled toilets available
BLIND : **Facilities Available**: No Special Facilities
BOOKINGS : **Are Bookings Necessary**: Yes **CONTACT NUMBER**: (0462) 434483

KINGSTONIAN FC

WHEELCHAIRS : **Location of Accommodation**: Accommodated around Ground
Nº Spaces for Home Fans; Nº Spaces for Away Fans: Not specified
Are Helpers Admitted; Nº Admitted: No limit to number of helpers admitted
PRICES : **Prices for Disabled; Prices for Helpers**: Normal prices for both the disabled and helpers
TOILETS : **Location of Disabled Toilets (+ Number)**: Disabled toilets available
BLIND : **Facilities Available**: No Special Facilities
BOOKINGS : **Are Bookings Necessary**: Yes **CONTACT NUMBER**: (081) 547-3335

Marlow FC

Wheelchairs : **Location of Accommodation**: No special accommodation, but disabled visitors welcome
Nº Spaces for Home Fans; Nº Spaces for Away Fans: -
Are Helpers Admitted; Nº Admitted: -
Prices : **Prices for Disabled; Prices for Helpers**: Normal prices
Toilets : **Location of Disabled Toilets (+ Number)**: None
Blind : **Facilities Available**: No Special Facilities
Bookings : **Are Bookings Necessary**: No **Contact Number**: (0528) 483970

Molesey FC

Wheelchairs : **Location of Accommodation**: Accommodated around Ground
Nº Spaces for Home Fans; Away Fans: Not specified
Are Helpers Admitted; Nº Admitted: Yes
Prices : **Prices for Disabled; Prices for Helpers**: Normal prices for both the disabled and helpers
Toilets : **Location of Disabled Toilets (+ Number)**: Disabled toilets available
Blind : **Facilities Available**: No Special Facilities
Bookings : **Are Bookings Necessary**: Yes **Contact Number**: (081) 979-4823

Purfleet FC

Wheelchairs : **Location of Accommodation**: No special accommodation, but wheelchairs are welcome
Nº Spaces for Home Fans; Nº Spaces for Away Fans: Not specified
Are Helpers Admitted; Nº Admitted: Yes
Prices : **Prices for Disabled; Prices for Helpers**: Normal prices for both the disabled and helpers
Toilets : **Location of Disabled Toilets (+ Number)**: Available in Hotel
Blind : **Facilities Available**: No Special Facilities
Bookings : **Are Bookings Necessary**: Yes **Contact Number**: (0708) 868901

St. Albans City FC

Wheelchairs : **Location of Accommodation**: Accommodated in front of the Main Stand
Nº Spaces for Home Fans; Nº Spaces for Away Fans: 6 spaces each for home & away fans
Are Helpers Admitted; Nº Admitted: One helper admitted per disabled supporter
Prices : **Prices for Disabled; Prices for Helpers**: £3.00 for the disabled. £4.50 for helpers
Toilets : **Location of Disabled Toilets (+ Number)**: None at present
Blind : **Facilities Available**: No Special Facilities
Bookings : **Are Bookings Necessary**: No **Contact Number**: (0727) 834920

Slough Town FC

Wheelchairs : **Location of Accommodation**: Accommodated in front of the Stand
Nº Spaces for Home Fans; Nº Spaces for Away Fans: 10 spaces each for home & away fans
Are Helpers Admitted; Nº Admitted: One helper admitted per disabled supporter
Prices : **Prices for Disabled; Prices for Helpers**: Normal prices for the disabled and helpers
Toilets : **Location of Disabled Toilets (+ Number)**: One available inside the Clubhouse
Blind : **Facilities Available**: No Special Facilities
Bookings : **Are Bookings Necessary**: Yes **Contact Number**: (0753) 523358

Sutton United FC

Wheelchairs : **Location of Accommodation**: Accommodated on track perimeter
Nº Spaces for Home Fans; Nº Spaces for Away Fans: 6 spaces each for home & away fans
Are Helpers Admitted; Nº Admitted: One helper admitted per disabled supporter
Prices : **Prices for Disabled; Prices for Helpers**: £2.00 each for both the disabled and the helpers
Toilets : **Location of Disabled Toilets (+ Number)**: One available alongside the Standing Terrace
Blind : **Facilities Available**: No Special facilities
Bookings : **Are Bookings Necessary**: Yes **Contact Number**: (081) 644-4440

Walton & Hersham FC

Wheelchairs : **Location of Accommodation**: Accommodated around Ground
Nº Spaces for Home Fans; Nº Spaces for Away Fans: Not specified
Are Helpers Admitted; Nº Admitted: Yes
Prices : **Prices for Disabled; Prices for Helpers**: Concessionary prices for disabled. Usual price helpers
Toilets : **Location of Disabled Toilets (+ Number)**: None
Blind : **Facilities Available**: No Special Facilities
Bookings : **Are Bookings Necessary**: Yes **Contact Number**: (0932) 245263

Wokingham Town FC

Wheelchairs : **Location of Accommodation**: Accommodated by the Centre Line
Nº Spaces for Home Fans; Nº Spaces for Away Fans: 6 spaces available in total
Are Helpers Admitted; Nº Admitted: Number of helpers admitted not specified
Prices : **Prices for Disabled; Prices for Helpers**: £3.50 each for both the disabled and the helpers
Toilets : **Location of Disabled Toilets (+ Number)**: None
Blind : **Facilities Available**: No Special Facilities
Bookings : **Are Bookings Necessary**: Advisable **Contact Number**: (0734) 780253

Yeading FC

Wheelchairs : **Location of Accommodation**: No special facilities for the disabled
Nº Spaces for Home Fans; Nº Spaces for Away Fans: Not specified
Are Helpers Admitted; Nº Admitted: -
Prices : **Prices for Disabled; Prices for Helpers**: -
Toilets : **Location of Disabled Toilets (+ Number)**: None
Blind : **Facilities Available**: No Special Facilities
Bookings : **Are Bookings Necessary**: No **Contact Number**: (081) 848-7362

Beazer Homes League Premier Division Clubs

Atherstone United FC

Wheelchairs : **Location of Accommodation**: Accommodated in the Centre Stand
Nº Spaces for Home Fans; Nº Spaces for Away Fans: 4 spaces available in total
Are Helpers Admitted; Nº Admitted: One helper admitted for each wheelchair
Prices : **Prices for Disabled; Prices for Helpers**: £3.50 for both the disabled and the helpers
Toilets : **Location of Disabled Toilets (+ Number)**: One available nearby
Blind : **Facilities Available**: No Special Facilities
Bookings : **Are Bookings Necessary**: Yes **Contact Number**: (0203) 349987

Burton Albion FC

Wheelchairs : **Location of Accommodation**: Accommodated at the far side of the Main Stand
Nº Spaces for Home Fans; Nº Spaces for Away Fans: 5 spaces each for home & away fans
Are Helpers Admitted; Nº Admitted: As many helpers are admitted as necessary
Prices : **Prices for Disabled; Prices for Helpers**: Reduced price for disabled. Normal price for helpers
Toilets : **Location of Disabled Toilets (+ Number)**: One available
Blind : **Facilities Available**: No Special Facilities
Bookings : **Are Bookings Necessary**: Helpful **Contact Number**: (0283) 65938

Cambridge City FC

Wheelchairs : **Location of Accommodation**: Accommodated on Stand Side, School End
Nº Spaces for Home Fans; Nº Spaces for Away Fans: 6 spaces available in total
Are Helpers Admitted; Nº Admitted: One helper admitted per disabled supporter
Prices : **Prices for Disabled; Prices for Helpers**: Free of charge for disabled. Normal price for helpers
Toilets : **Location of Disabled Toilets (+ Number)**: One available in the centre of the Main Stand
Blind : **Facilities Available**: No Special Facilities
Bookings : **Are Bookings Necessary**: No **Contact Number**: (0223) 357973

Chelmsford City FC

Wheelchairs : **Location of Accommodation**: Accommodated via Wolseley End
Nº Spaces for Home Fans; Nº Spaces for Away Fans: Not specified
Are Helpers Admitted; Nº Admitted: Yes
Prices : **Prices for Disabled; Prices for Helpers**: Normal prices for both the disabled and helpers
Toilets : **Location of Disabled Toilets (+ Number)**: None
Blind : **Facilities Available**: No Special Facilities
Bookings : **Are Bookings Necessary**: Yes **Contact Number**: (0245) 353052

Cheltenham Town FC

Wheelchairs : **Location of Accommodation**: Accommodated around Ground
Nº Spaces for Home Fans; Nº Spaces for Away Fans: Not specified
Are Helpers Admitted; Nº Admitted: Yes
Prices : **Prices for Disabled; Prices for Helpers**: Normal prices for both the disabled and helpers
Toilets : **Location of Disabled Toilets (+ Number)**: None
Blind : **Facilities Available**: No Special Facilities
Bookings : **Are Bookings Necessary**: Yes **Contact Number**: (0242) 573558

Corby Town FC

Wheelchairs : **Location of Accommodation**: Accommodated in front of the Main Stand
Nº Spaces for Home Fans; Nº Spaces for Away Fans: 2 spaces each for home & away fans
Are Helpers Admitted; Nº Admitted: No helpers admitted
Prices : **Prices for Disabled; Prices for Helpers**: £4.00 for the disabled
Toilets : **Location of Disabled Toilets (+ Number)**: One available alongside the toilets under the Stand
Blind : **Facilities Available**: No Special Facilities
Bookings : **Are Bookings Necessary**: No **Contact Number**: (0536) 406604

Crawley Town FC

Wheelchairs : **Location of Accommodation**: Accommodated in Disabled area in Main Stand
Nº Spaces for Home Fans; Nº Spaces for Away Fans: No limit (within reason)
Are Helpers Admitted; Nº Admitted: Yes
Prices : **Prices for Disabled; Prices for Helpers**: Normal prices for both the disabled and helpers
Toilets : **Location of Disabled Toilets (+ Number)**: Disabled toilets available
Blind : **Facilities Available**: Help available by arrangement
Bookings : **Are Bookings Necessary**: No **Contact Number**: (0293) 542718

Dorchester Town FC

Wheelchairs : **Location of Accommodation**: Accommodated at the North West end of the Terracing
Nº Spaces for Home Fans; Nº Spaces for Away Fans: 10 spaces each for home & away fans
Are Helpers Admitted; Nº Admitted: Maximum of 10 helpers admitted
Prices : **Prices for Disabled; Prices for Helpers**: £3.70 each for the disabled and helpers
Toilets : **Location of Disabled Toilets (+ Number)**: 2 available near the disabled area
Blind : **Facilities Available**: No Special Facilities
Bookings : **Are Bookings Necessary**: No **Contact Number**: (0305) 262451

Gloucester City FC

Wheelchairs : **Location of Accommodation**: Accommodated alongside the Main Stand
Nº Spaces for Home Fans; Nº Spaces for Away Fans: 6 spaces each for home & away fans
Are Helpers Admitted; Nº Admitted: One helper admitted per disabled supporter
Prices : **Prices for Disabled; Prices for Helpers**: Concessionary rate charged for the disabled & helpers
Toilets : **Location of Disabled Toilets (+ Number)**: 2 in main toilet block + 1 on other side of ground
Blind : **Facilities Available**: No Special Facilities
Bookings : **Are Bookings Necessary**: Yes **Contact Number**: (0252) 522514

Gravesend & Northfleet FC

Wheelchairs : **Location of Accommodation**: Disabled area - in front of Main Stand
Nº Spaces for Home Fans; Nº Spaces for Away Fans: 6 spaces available in total
Are Helpers Admitted; Nº Admitted: Yes
Prices : **Prices for Disabled; Prices for Helpers**: Half-price for the disabled. Full price for helpers
Toilets : **Location of Disabled Toilets (+ Number)**: Disabled toilets available
Blind : **Facilities Available**: No Special Facilities
Bookings : **Are Bookings Necessary**: No **Contact Number**: (0474) 363424

Gresley Rovers FC

Wheelchairs : **Location of Accommodation**: No specific area, but can be accommodated
Nº Spaces for Home Fans; Nº Spaces for Away Fans: Not specified
Are Helpers Admitted; Nº Admitted: One helper admitted per disabled supporter
Prices : **Prices for Disabled; Prices for Helpers**: Normal prices for both the disabled and helpers
Toilets : **Location of Disabled Toilets (+ Number)**: None
Blind : **Facilities Available**: No Special Facilities
Bookings : **Are Bookings Necessary**: No **Contact Number**: (0283) 221881

Halesowen Town FC

Wheelchairs : **Location of Accommodation**: Accommodated to each side of the Main Seating Stand
Nº Spaces for Home Fans; Nº Spaces for Away Fans: 20 spaces available in total
Are Helpers Admitted; Nº Admitted: No limit on the number of helpers (within reason)
Prices : **Prices for Disabled; Prices for Helpers**: Free of charge for the disabled. £3.30 for helpers
Toilets : **Location of Disabled Toilets (+ Number)**: Located 25 yards from the Main Seating Stand
Blind : **Facilities Available**: No Special Facilities
Bookings : **Are Bookings Necessary**: No **Contact Number**: (021) 550-2179

Hastings Town FC

Wheelchairs : **Location of Accommodation**: Arrangements can be made if notified in advance
Nº Spaces for Home Fans; Nº Spaces for Away Fans: Not specified
Are Helpers Admitted; Nº Admitted: No limit on the number of helpers (within reason)
Prices : **Prices for Disabled; Prices for Helpers**: £3.50 or £2.00 for the disabled. Free for helpers
Toilets : **Location of Disabled Toilets (+ Number)**: None
Blind : **Facilities Available**: No Special Facilities
Bookings : **Are Bookings Necessary**: Yes **Contact Number**: (0424) 444635

Hednesford Town FC

Wheelchairs : **Location of Accommodation**: Front of Boardroom, between the goal-line and halfway-line
Nº Spaces for Home Fans; Nº Spaces for Away Fans: 10 spaces available in total
Are Helpers Admitted; Nº Admitted: One helper admitted per disabled supporter
Prices : **Prices for Disabled; Prices for Helpers**: £1.70 for the disabled. £3.40 for helpers
Toilets : **Location of Disabled Toilets (+ Number)**: None
Blind : **Facilities Available**: No Special Facilities
Bookings : **Are Bookings Necessary**: Preferable **Contact Number**: (0543) 876887

Rushden Diamonds FC

Wheelchairs : **Location of Accommodation**: Accommodated around Ground
Nº Spaces for Home Fans; Nº Spaces for Away Fans: Not specified
Are Helpers Admitted; Nº Admitted: Yes
Prices : **Prices for Disabled; Prices for Helpers**: Normal prices for both the disabled and helpers
Toilets : **Location of Disabled Toilets (+ Number)**: Not stated
Blind : **Facilities Available**: No Special Facilities
Bookings : **Are Bookings Necessary**: Yes **Contact Number**: (0933) 650345

Sittingbourne FC

Wheelchairs : **Location of Accommodation**: Accommodated in Main Stand and on Terraces
Nº Spaces for Home Fans; Nº Spaces for Away Fans: 20 spaces for home fans; 10 for away
Are Helpers Admitted; Nº Admitted: One helper admitted per disabled supporters
Prices : **Prices for Disabled; Prices for Helpers**: £3.00 each for both the disabled and the helpers
Toilets : **Location of Disabled Toilets (+ Number)**: Two available within the Main Stand
Blind : **Facilities Available**: No Special Facilities
Bookings : **Are Bookings Necessary**: No **Contact Number**: (0795) 477547

Solihull Borough FC

Wheelchairs : **Location of Accommodation**: Accommodated in front of the Main Stand
Nº Spaces for Home Fans; Nº Spaces for Away Fans: Not specified
Are Helpers Admitted; Nº Admitted: One helper admitted for each wheelchair
Prices : **Prices for Disabled; Prices for Helpers**: Free of charge for both the disabled and helpers
Toilets : **Location of Disabled Toilets (+ Number)**: None
Blind : **Facilities Available**: No Special Facilities
Bookings : **Are Bookings Necessary**: No **Contact Number**: (021) 745-6758

Sudbury Town FC

Wheelchairs : **Location of Accommodation**: Accommodated around Ground
Nº Spaces for Home Fans; Nº Spaces for Away Fans: Not specified
Are Helpers Admitted; Nº Admitted: Yes
Prices : **Prices for Disabled; Prices for Helpers**: Normal prices for both the disabled and helpers
Toilets : **Location of Disabled Toilets (+ Number)**: None
Blind : **Facilities Available**: No Special Facilities
Bookings : **Are Bookings Necessary**: Yes **Contact Number**: (0787) 379095

Trowbridge Town FC

Wheelchairs : **Location of Accommodation**: Accommodated in front of the Main Stand
Nº Spaces for Home Fans; Nº Spaces for Away Fans: 10 spaces each for home & away fans
Are Helpers Admitted; Nº Admitted: One helper admitted per disabled supporter
Prices : **Prices for Disabled; Prices for Helpers**: £2.50 each for the disabled. £2.00 each for helpers
Toilets : **Location of Disabled Toilets (+ Number)**: None
Blind : **Facilities Available**: No Special Facilities
Bookings : **Are Bookings Necessary**: No **Contact Number**: (0225) 767187

V. S. Rugby FC

Wheelchairs : **Location of Accommodation**: Accommodated near the Main Stand
Nº Spaces for Home Fans; Nº Spaces for Away Fans: No specific number
Are Helpers Admitted; Nº Admitted: Yes
Prices : **Prices for Disabled; Prices for Helpers**: Normal prices for both the disabled and helpers
Toilets : **Location of Disabled Toilets (+ Number)**: None
Blind : **Facilities Available**: Commentaries may be available. Phone for details
Bookings : **Are Bookings Necessary**: Yes **Contact Number**: (0788) 543692

Witton Albion FC

Wheelchairs : **Location of Accommodation**: Accommodated at the Wincham End of the Grandstand
Nº Spaces for Home Fans; Nº Spaces for Away Fans: 6 spaces each for home & away fans
Are Helpers Admitted; Nº Admitted: One helper admitted per wheelchair
Prices : **Prices for Disabled; Prices for Helpers**: £5.00 or £3.50 each for both disabled and helpers
Toilets : **Location of Disabled Toilets (+ Number)**: One available at the End of the Stand
Blind : **Facilities Available**: No Special Facilities
Bookings : **Are Bookings Necessary**: Yes **Contact Number**: (0606) 43008

Worcester City FC

Wheelchairs : **Location of Accommodation**: Accommodated by arrangement
Nº Spaces for Home Fans; Nº Spaces for Away Fans: Not specified
Are Helpers Admitted; Nº Admitted: Yes
Prices : **Prices for Disabled; Prices for Helpers**: Normal prices for both the disabled and helpers
Toilets : **Location of Disabled Toilets (+ Number)**: None
Blind : **Facilities Available**: No Special Facilities
Bookings : **Are Bookings Necessary**: Yes **Contact Number**: (0905) 23003

Northern Premier League Premier Division

Accrington Stanley FC

Wheelchairs : **Location of Accommodation**: No specific areas, but can be accommodated by arrangement
Nº Spaces for Home Fans; Nº Spaces for Away Fans: Not specified
Are Helpers Admitted; Nº Admitted: Not specified
Prices : **Prices for Disabled; Prices for Helpers**: Normal prices apply
Toilets : **Location of Disabled Toilets (+ Number)**: None
Blind : **Facilities Available**: No Special Facilities
Bookings : **Are Bookings Necessary**: Yes **Contact Number**: (0254) 383235

Barrow AFC

Wheelchairs : **Location of Accommodation**: Accommodated by arrangement
Nº Spaces for Home Fans; Nº Spaces for Away Fans: Not specified
Are Helpers Admitted; Nº Admitted: Yes
Prices : **Prices for Disabled; Prices for Helpers**: Normal prices for both the disabled and helpers
Toilets : **Location of Disabled Toilets (+ Number)**: None
Blind : **Facilities Available**: No Special Facilities
Bookings : **Are Bookings Necessary**: Yes **Contact Number**: (0229) 820346

BISHOP AUCKLAND FC

WHEELCHAIRS : **Location of Accommodation**: No specific area
Nº Spaces for Home Fans; Nº Spaces for Away Fans: Not specified
Are Helpers Admitted; Nº Admitted: Helpers are admitted
PRICES : **Prices for Disabled; Prices for Helpers**: Helpers free if Secretary contacted in advance
TOILETS : **Location of Disabled Toilets (+ Number)**: None
BLIND : **Facilities Available**: No Special Facilities
BOOKINGS : **Are Bookings Necessary**: No **CONTACT NUMBER**: (0388) 608330

BOSTON UNITED FC

WHEELCHAIRS : **Location of Accommodation**: Accommodated at the York Street End
Nº Spaces for Home Fans; Nº Spaces for Away Fans: 5 spaces each for home & away fans
Are Helpers Admitted; Nº Admitted: One helper admitted for each wheelchair
PRICES : **Prices for Disabled; Prices for Helpers**: £2.50 each for the disabled and helpers
TOILETS : **Location of Disabled Toilets (+ Number)**: None
BLIND : **Facilities Available**: No Special Facilities
BOOKINGS : **Are Bookings Necessary**: Appreciated **CONTACT NUMBER**: (0205) 364406

BUXTON FC

WHEELCHAIRS : **Location of Accommodation**: Accommodated by arrangement
Nº Spaces for Home Fans; Nº Spaces for Away Fans: No specific spaces
Are Helpers Admitted; Nº Admitted: Yes
PRICES : **Prices for Disabled; Prices for Helpers**: Free of charge for both the disabled and helpers
TOILETS : **Location of Disabled Toilets (+ Number)**: Disabled toilets available
BLIND : **Facilities Available**: No Special Facilities
BOOKINGS : **Are Bookings Necessary**: Yes **CONTACT NUMBER**: (0298) 26033

CHORLEY FC

WHEELCHAIRS : **Location of Accommodation**: Accommodated by arrangement
Nº Spaces for Home Fans; Nº Spaces for Away Fans: No specific spaces
Are Helpers Admitted; Nº Admitted: Yes
PRICES : **Prices for Disabled; Prices for Helpers**: Normal prices for both the disabled and helpers
TOILETS : **Location of Disabled Toilets (+ Number)**: None
BLIND : **Facilities Available**: No Special Facilities
BOOKINGS : **Are Bookings Necessary**: Yes **CONTACT NUMBER**: (0772) 719266

COLWYN BAY FC

WHEELCHAIRS : **Location of Accommodation**: Accommodated in covered terrace
Nº Spaces for Home Fans; Nº Spaces for Away Fans: Not specified
Are Helpers Admitted; Nº Admitted: Yes
PRICES : **Prices for Disabled; Prices for Helpers**: Free of charge for disabled. Normal prices helpers
TOILETS : **Location of Disabled Toilets (+ Number)**: None
BLIND : **Facilities Available**: No Special Facilities
BOOKINGS : **Are Bookings Necessary**: No **CONTACT NUMBER**: (0492) 516941

DROYLESDEN FC

WHEELCHAIRS : **Location of Accommodation**: Accommodated beside the Stand
Nº Spaces for Home Fans; Nº Spaces for Away Fans: No specific number
Are Helpers Admitted; Nº Admitted: Yes
PRICES : **Prices for Disabled; Prices for Helpers**: Normal prices for both the disabled and helpers
TOILETS : **Location of Disabled Toilets (+ Number)**: Disabled toilets available
BLIND : **Facilities Available**: No Special Facilities
BOOKINGS : **Are Bookings Necessary**: Yes **CONTACT NUMBER**: (061) 370-1426

EMLEY FC

WHEELCHAIRS : **Location of Accommodation**: Accommodated in front of the Main Stand
Nº Spaces for Home Fans; Nº Spaces for Away Fans: 3 spaces for home fans; 2 for away
Are Helpers Admitted; Nº Admitted: One helper admitted per wheelchair
PRICES : **Prices for Disabled; Prices for Helpers**: £3.50 each for both the disabled and helpers
TOILETS : **Location of Disabled Toilets (+ Number)**: One Ladies and one Gents
BLIND : **Facilities Available**: No Special Facilities
BOOKINGS : **Are Bookings Necessary**: No **CONTACT NUMBER**: (0924) 840087 or 848398

Frickley Athletic FC

Wheelchairs : **Location of Accommodation**: Accommodated within Perimeter Wall
Nº Spaces for Home Fans; Nº Spaces for Away Fans: Not specified
Are Helpers Admitted; Nº Admitted: Yes
Prices : **Prices for Disabled; Prices for Helpers**: Normal prices for both the disabled and helpers
Toilets : **Location of Disabled Toilets (+ Number)**: Available in Stand
Blind : **Facilities Available**: No Special Facilities
Bookings : **Are Bookings Necessary**: No **Contact Number**: (0977) 643316

Gainsborough Town FC

Wheelchairs : **Location of Accommodation**: No special area, but can be accommodated around Ground
Nº Spaces for Home Fans; Nº Spaces for Away Fans: Not specified
Are Helpers Admitted; Nº Admitted: Yes
Prices : **Prices for Disabled; Prices for Helpers**: Usual prices for the disabled and helpers
Toilets : **Location of Disabled Toilets (+ Number)**: None
Blind : **Facilities Available**: No Special Facilities
Bookings : **Are Bookings Necessary**: No **Contact Number**: (0427) 615625 or 613295

Guiseley FC

Wheelchairs : **Location of Accommodation**: Accommodated by Players' Entrance
Nº Spaces for Home Fans; Nº Spaces for Away Fans: No specific number
Are Helpers Admitted; Nº Admitted: Yes
Prices : **Prices for Disabled; Prices for Helpers**: Free of charge for disabled. Normal prices for helpers
Toilets : **Location of Disabled Toilets (+ Number)**: None
Blind : **Facilities Available**: No Special Facilities
Bookings : **Are Bookings Necessary**: Yes **Contact Number**: (0943) 872872

Horwich R.M.I. FC

Wheelchairs : **Location of Accommodation**: No specific area, but accommodated around the Ground
Nº Spaces for Home Fans; Nº Spaces for Away Fans: No fixed number
Are Helpers Admitted; Nº Admitted: Helpers admitted as required
Prices : **Prices for Disabled; Prices for Helpers**: Usually full price for both the disabled and helpers
Toilets : **Location of Disabled Toilets (+ Number)**: None
Blind : **Facilities Available**: No Special Facilities
Bookings : **Are Bookings Necessary**: No **Contact Number**: (0204) 696908

Hyde United FC

Wheelchairs : **Location of Accommodation**: No specific area, but accommodated around the Ground
Nº Spaces for Home Fans; Nº Spaces for Away Fans: Not specified
Are Helpers Admitted; Nº Admitted: Not specified
Prices : **Prices for Disabled; Prices for Helpers**: Normal prices
Toilets : **Location of Disabled Toilets (+ Number)**: None
Blind : **Facilities Available**: No Special Facilities
Bookings : **Are Bookings Necessary**: No **Contact Number**: (061) 368-3687

Knowsley United FC

Wheelchairs : **Location of Accommodation**: Accommodated behind the goal to the left and right
Nº Spaces for Home Fans; Nº Spaces for Away Fans: 4 spaces each for home & away fans
Are Helpers Admitted; Nº Admitted: Maximum of 4 helpers admitted
Prices : **Prices for Disabled; Prices for Helpers**: £2.00 each for both the disabled and the helpers
Toilets : **Location of Disabled Toilets (+ Number)**: Two available inside complex
Blind : **Facilities Available**: No Special Facilities
Bookings : **Are Bookings Necessary**: No **Contact Number**: (051) 474-3808

Leek Town FC

Wheelchairs : **Location of Accommodation**: Not specified
Nº Spaces for Home Fans; Nº Spaces for Away Fans: 5 spaces for home fans; 4 for away
Are Helpers Admitted; Nº Admitted: One helper admitted for each wheelchair
Prices : **Prices for Disabled; Prices for Helpers**: Normal prices for the disabled and helpers
Toilets : **Location of Disabled Toilets (+ Number)**: 1 available by each of the disabled areas
Blind : **Facilities Available**: No Special Facilities
Bookings : **Are Bookings Necessary**: Yes **Contact Number**: (0538) 399276

MARINE FC

WHEELCHAIRS : **Location of Accommodation**: Accommodated in front of the Stand
Nº Spaces for Home Fans; Nº Spaces for Away Fans: Not specified
Are Helpers Admitted; Nº Admitted: Yes
PRICES : **Prices for Disabled; Prices for Helpers**: Normal prices for both the disabled and helpers
TOILETS : **Location of Disabled Toilets (+ Number)**: None
BLIND : **Facilities Available**: No Special Facilities
BOOKINGS : **Are Bookings Necessary**: No **CONTACT NUMBER**: (051) 924-1743

MATLOCK TOWN FC

WHEELCHAIRS : **Location of Accommodation**: No specific area, but accommodated around the Ground
Nº Spaces for Home Fans; Nº Spaces for Away Fans: No limit (within reason)
Are Helpers Admitted; Nº Admitted: No practical limit to number of helpers
PRICES : **Prices for Disabled; Prices for Helpers**: Free of charge for the disabled. Normal price helpers
TOILETS : **Location of Disabled Toilets (+ Number)**: One in the corner of the Ground with Main Toilets
BLIND : **Facilities Available**: No Special Facilities
BOOKINGS : **Are Bookings Necessary**: No **CONTACT NUMBER**: (0629) 583866

MORECAMBE FC

WHEELCHAIRS : **Location of Accommodation**: Accommodated on Approach to Main Stand
Nº Spaces for Home Fans; Nº Spaces for Away Fans: 10 spaces available in total
Are Helpers Admitted; Nº Admitted: Maximum of 10 helpers admitted
PRICES : **Prices for Disabled; Prices for Helpers**: Full prices for the disabled and helpers
TOILETS : **Location of Disabled Toilets (+ Number)**: To be built during Summer 1994
BLIND : **Facilities Available**: No Special Facilities
BOOKINGS : **Are Bookings Necessary**: No **CONTACT NUMBER**: (0524) 833358

SPENNYMOOR UNITED FC

WHEELCHAIRS : **Location of Accommodation**: Accommodated by arrangement
Nº Spaces for Home Fans; Nº Spaces for Away Fans: No specific number
Are Helpers Admitted; Nº Admitted: Yes
PRICES : **Prices for Disabled; Prices for Helpers**: Normal prices for both the disabled and helpers
TOILETS : **Location of Disabled Toilets (+ Number)**: Available in Clubhouse
BLIND : **Facilities Available**: No Special Facilities
BOOKINGS : **Are Bookings Necessary**: Yes **CONTACT NUMBER**: (0388) 811934

WHITLEY BAY FC

WHEELCHAIRS : **Location of Accommodation**: Accommodated in the Front of the Stand - under cover
Nº Spaces for Home Fans; Nº Spaces for Away Fans: 20 spaces available in total
Are Helpers Admitted; Nº Admitted: One helper admitted per disabled supporter
PRICES : **Prices for Disabled; Prices for Helpers**: £1.75 each for the disabled and helpers
TOILETS : **Location of Disabled Toilets (+ Number)**: None
BLIND : **Facilities Available**: Help available at Ground, but otherwise no special facilities
BOOKINGS : **Are Bookings Necessary**: If possible **CONTACT NUMBER**: (091) 251-5179

WINSFORD UNITED FC

WHEELCHAIRS : **Location of Accommodation**: Accommodated beside the Main Stand
Nº Spaces for Home Fans; Nº Spaces for Away Fans: No specific number
Are Helpers Admitted; Nº Admitted: Yes
PRICES : **Prices for Disabled; Prices for Helpers**: Prices charged at the discretion of the Club
TOILETS : **Location of Disabled Toilets (+ Number)**: None
BLIND : **Facilities Available**: No Special Facilities
BOOKINGS : **Are Bookings Necessary**: Yes **CONTACT NUMBER**: (0606) 861980

The Supporters' Guides : -

THE SUPPORTERS' GUIDE TO PREMIER & FOOTBALL LEAGUE CLUBS 1995

Featuring :
- all F.A. Carling Premiership clubs
- all Football League clubs

+ Results, tables

112 pages - price £4.99

THE SUPPORTERS' GUIDE TO NON-LEAGUE FOOTBALL 1995

Featuring :
- all GM/Vauxhall Conference clubs
- all Northern Premier clubs
- all Beazer Homes - Premier clubs
- all Diadora Premier clubs

+ 180 other major Non-League clubs

112 pages - price £4.99

THE SUPPORTERS' GUIDE TO SCOTTISH FOOTBALL 1995

Featuring :
- all Scottish League clubs
- all Highland League clubs
- all East & South of Scotland League clubs

+ Results, tables

96 pages - price £4.99

THE SUPPORTERS' GUIDE TO WELSH FOOTBALL 1995

Featuring :
- all Konica League of Wales clubs
- all Cymru Alliance clubs
- all Welsh Football League clubs

+ 'The Exiles', Minor League clubs & 1993/94 season's results and tables

96 pages - price £4.99

As a special offer to Shoot Disabled Supporters' Guide readers, the guides shown are available priced at only £4.00 each - *post free. Order from :*

Soccer Book Publishing Ltd.
Department SDSG
72 St. Peters Avenue,
Cleethorpes
South Humberside
DN35 8HU